A PARLIAMENT OF OWLS

A Bird Watchers Mystery

CHRIS GOFF

CONTENTS

A PARLIAMENT OF OWLS

Chapter 1

Angela Dimato saw the crowd waiting for her in front of the Rocky Mountain Arsenal's Visitor Center and briefly considered turning around. She counted several adults and at least a dozen middle-schoolers, ages twelve to fourteen. Not exactly her idea of a fun morning of birding, and not that she didn't like kids. She just hated being outnumbered.

Swinging the U.S. Fish and Wildlife truck into a VIP parking spot, she cut the motor and reached for her duty belt. She might be playing tour guide this morning, but she was still a U. S. Fish and Wildlife Special Agent. She cinched on the belt, checked to make sure her gun was secured, and then reached back behind the seat for her binoculars and spotting scope. Through the passenger window, she caught sight of her boss, Wayne Canon, walking toward her and waving.

"Good, you're here," he called out. "I brought some gear over for the kids and their teachers. They're ready to go."

Angela climbed out of the truck and tucked a birding guide into her back pocket. "You owe me, Canon."

"Trust me, I know," Wayne said. As the Special Agent in Charge of Law Enforcement for USFW's Region 6, he'd also been acting Project Director for the Rocky Mountain Arsenal National Wildlife Refuge Complex for the past month. The complex was a group of three national wildlife refuges along the Front Range. He was in over his head. Over worked and under staffed, Wayne had pulled Angela out of the field and assigned her to the National Eagle and Wildlife Property Repositories.

Recovering from the death of her partner in January, Angela liked working to make a dent in the $23 billion illegal wildlife product industry. She didn't like babysitting tourists. And asking her to lead a Monday-morning summer school class on a birding tour of the Refuge fell way outside of her purview.

"You owe me <u>big</u>."

Wayne glanced over his shoulder at the group and lowered his voice. "I wouldn't have asked you to cover if I had anyone else. I have two agents out and our usual go-to called in sick. I'll make it up to you, Dimato. I promise."

Famous last words, but it was a chit she intended to collect.

Angela's gaze swept the sun-drenched prairie. In the distance, the Continental Divide cut a purple swatch across the clear blue sky, beckoning with the promise of cooler temperatures. At seven-thirty a.m., it had already climbed to seventy-two degrees on the plains and promised to be one of the hottest July days on record.

"I'll bet you that your 'go-to' girl got up and went to the mountains," Angela said.

"Yeah, well, she's going to up and get hers before it's all said and done." Wayne took the scope from Angela's hand, and gestured for her to follow. "Come on, I'll introduce you to Tammy Crawford. She's the group leader."

Angela dogged his heels, sizing Crawford up as they approached. Contrasting the schoolteacher's tank top, cotton shorts and lace-up tennis shoes against her own short-sleeved rough-duty shirt, long pants and sturdy boots, Angela determined they were exact opposites. Where Crawford was tall and fair, with a smile that made fifty percent of her young charges swoon, Angela's biggest draw was her gun.

"I'm so pleased to meet you, Agent Dimato," Crawford said, thrusting out a hand. "Wayne was just telling us how lucky we are that you're the one who's going to be showing us around."

Angela's resolve to dislike Crawford thawed under the wattage of the teacher's smile, and she found herself smiling back. "Canon told me you're interested in having the kids see some birds."

"And learn something about the Arsenal. I teach biology, but my colleague, Mr. Burton, teaches history." Crawford gestured toward an older gentleman, who was attempting to corral a trio of rambunctious boys. "We run the summer school program at Commerce City Academy."

Angela shot a glance at Wayne. The fact they were part of the Academy explained a lot about why he wanted someone knowledgeable leading the tour. Maintaining positive relationships with Commerce City was high on the Refuge's to-do list.

In 1992, when the Rocky Mountain Arsenal National Wildlife Refuge Act was signed, the primary stated objectives of the agreement were restoring and managing the land to provide quality wildlife habitat and providing environmental education programs for urban school children. 917 acres had been annexed to Commerce City to help pay for the new Visitors Center and provide for road expansion and development around the perimeter of the Refuge. The city built a high school, several government buildings and Dick's Sporting Goods Park on the acquired land. Now, Commerce City Academy was the newest addition, the crown jewel in the city's new educational program.

"I leave you in good hands," Canon said.

When he was done saying his goodbyes and had walked away, Angela turned to Crawford. No point in putting things off. "I suggest that we get started. Why don't you gather the troops, and we'll head inside."

While Crawford and Burton rounded up the children, Angela unlocked the Visitors Center and flipped on the lights. It didn't officially open for another hour, which left plenty of time for a private tour.

Angela thought about Ian, as she waited for the kids to line up at the door. Her partner had loved children. He had been murdered just months before he planned to retire. Forced out of service by a heart condition, she had asked him what he planned to do next. He'd told her he wanted to teach. Maybe today she could channel his spirit.

Leading the kids inside, she gestured for them to sit in a semi-circle on the floor of the lobby. "We'll start in here."

Angela pointed to a circle of exhibits behind her. The dioramas and displays detailed the early times on the plains, the history of the Refuge and provided animal visuals and hands-on exhibits. One of the boys she'd seen Burton struggle with earlier made a face.

"Why do we have to look at a lame museum?" he asked.

"Leroy, be quiet," Mr. Burton said.

Ms. Crawford smiled. "Continue, Agent Dimato."

"But you said we were going to spend the day outside." Leroy wasn't that easy to dissuade.

Ms. Crawford looked at the boy. "Didn't Mr. Burton ask you to be quiet?"

"Yes, Ma'am."

"Then be quiet." Ms. Crawford beamed at Angela. "Go ahead, Agent."

Angela felt like she was in school standing in front of her classmates and teacher, giving a report. Her insides trembled. Speaking in front of a group had never come easy. And, despite the fact she was a college-graduate standing in front of a group of twelve year-olds, this was no exception.

"There are some cool things to learn about the Rocky Mountain Arsenal," she started. "It wasn't always a wildlife refuge."

"What was it?" asked a girl with strawberry blond braids.

"It started out as short-grass prairie, when large herds of bison roamed the plains." Angela pointed at a stuffed bison marking the exhibit entrance. "American Indians followed the herds, hunting and living off the land. Later, settlers moved west and homesteaded here, growing crops and grazing cattle. Then, during World War II, the U.S. Army moved in and built a chemical weapons manufacturing facility called the Rocky Mountain Arsenal."

"What do you mean by 'chemical weapon?'?" Leroy asked.

Angela smiled. At least she had his attention. "They made bombs here and filled them with mustard gas, nerve agents and napalm."

"What's mustard gas?" asked the girl with the braids.

"What's napalm? Leroy asked.

Angela found herself at a loss for words. She wondered how graphic a description she was allowed to give. But, before she could answer, Mr. Burton stepped in.

"They're weapons of mass destruction," he said.

The answer seemed to satisfy the kids, so Angela continued. "Eventually the war ended and the plant was demilitarized."

"What's that mean?" asked another girl.

"The army shut down the operations," Mr. Burton said.

The kids all nodded.

Angela stared out at the faces and chose her next words carefully. "The chemicals they used to make the bombs were harmful—to the land, to people and to wildlife. That's why, in the 1980's, the Arsenal was named a Super Fund site."

"What's a Superfund site?"

Ms. Crawford interrupted. "Enough, Leroy! Let Agent Dimato finish."

Angela forced a smile. If she was being graded, she would be getting, at best, a C. "It's a site with abandoned hazardous materials that's been marked for cleanup. Designating it a Superfund site, gives the Environmental Protection Agency, the EPA, the right to come in and monitor the process."

"Like the mustard gas?" Leroy asked.

Angela nodded. "The EPA makes sure that immediate action is taken, enforces the laws against the responsible parties, ensures community involvement and ensures long-term protection. The Rocky Mountain Arsenal was made a Superfund site in 1987 and was named a National Wildlife Refuge in 1992. It's comprised of 17,000 acres, making it one of the largest urban wildlife refuges in the country."

Ms. Crawford looked out at the kids. "Does anyone have any questions for Agent Dimato?"

A volley of hands shot up.

"Is that a real gun?" Leroy shouted.

"Yes," Angela said. She knew it was her most interesting feature.

"Any questions about the Refuge," Ms. Crawford clarified.

"Did they get everything cleaned up?" Leroy asked.

"You've asked a question," Mr. Burton said. "And you need to wait your turn."

It was a good question, and Angela chose to answer. "Yes. They completed the cleanup in 2010."

"What did it cost?" asked a boy beside Leroy.

"$2.1 billion."

Crawford showed the boys her palm and nodded at a girl with dark eyes and an uneven haircut. "Amanda?"

"What kinds of animals live here?"

"Great question," Angela said. "Bison, mule deer, white-tailed deer, coyotes, prairie dogs and rabbits. Plus we have over 300 species of birds."

"What's a species?" Leroy blurted out.

"Types," Angela answered, already feeling tired.

"Are there any dangerous animals?" asked Amanda.

"All wild animals can be dangerous," Ms. Crawford said, then looked expectantly at Angela.

"The most dangerous creature we have isn't an animal. It's a reptile—the Western diamondback rattlesnake." Angela was pleased to see one or two of the kids' mouths drop open. "I'll be happy to answer more questions later, but right now I'm going to give you about twenty minutes to look around."

Before the words cleared her mouth, the kids were up and streaming toward the exhibits with Mr. Burton close on their heels.

"Thank you, Agent Dimato," Crawford said, standing and dusting off the front of her shorts.

Angela nodded. "Look, I need to make sure we have everything we need on the bus. Can you just make sure that the kids don't touch anything they're not supposed to? We especially don't want them climbing on the stuffed bison." She inclined her head toward the entrance to the exhibits, where one of Leroy's buddies was boosting him onto the back of the large, stuffed mammal.

Crawford moved quickly. "Leroy Henderson, you come down from there."

Thirty minutes later, after everyone had used the bathrooms and Angela had locked up, the kids and teachers were again gathered by the bus. The temperature had spiked to eighty degrees.

"Okay, listen up," Angela said. "It's getting hot, and we need to hurry if we want to see any animals. I'm going to loan each of you a set of binoculars."

"All right!" Leroy tried grabbing at the pair in her hands. Angela lifted them out of his reach.

"Just chill," she said, then immediately felt bad when all of his friends laughed. "Come here, you can help me demonstrate how to use them."

With Leroy as a guinea pig, she showed the others how to set the focus.

"That's so cool," Leroy said, sweeping the binoculars toward the prairie.

Angela grinned. The kid was smart.

"We'll pass out the binoculars as you get on the bus," Ms. Crawford said. "Let's line up."

Five minutes later, the kids were outfitted and seated on the bus. Angela climbed aboard and stood in the front near the driver.

"Before we head out, we need to cover some ground rules," she said. "We're going to drive into the Refuge and stop in the bison pasture. We are _not_ getting out. Bison are big, dangerous animals, so no shouting or screaming or trying to draw their attention. Got it?"

The kids all answered in the affirmative. Burton and Crawford nodded.

"Rule number two."

"What was rule number one?" Leroy asked.

Angela gave him a dirty look. Just when she was starting to like the kid, he had to come up with a smart ass question.

"Stay in the bus," she said. "You're allowed to get off, only when I tell you."

"Got it," Leroy said.

"Rule number two, keep your eyes open for wildlife. Again, never shout at them or try to feed them anything. We are visitors on their land."

"Got it," said the kids in unison, the chatter rising to ear shattering levels, until Ms. Crawford raised her hand. Angela nodded her thanks.

"After we're through the bison pasture, we're going to make a few stops. First, we'll head out to one of the best viewing sites of our premier prairie dog town. We'll get out there and see if we can spot any burrowing owls."

"Why do owls live—?"

Angela raised her hand, cutting Leroy off. "Bison first, then I'll tell you about the owls."

He nodded.

"When we're done looking at the burrowing owls, we'll head to the eagle watch." The platform for watching the roosting eagles in the winter and the nesting pair in the spring was only opened to visitors on special days or for private tours. The kids were in for a treat. "This year we have two fledglings—baby eagles," Angela said, anticipating the question. "Since it's nearing the middle of July, the eaglets are about to leave the nest and fly for the first time. With any luck, maybe we'll see it happen."

The kids broke into an excited chatter and Ms. Crawford banged on a seat back rail to quiet them down. "Let's listen to Agent Dimato," she said.

Once the noise subsided, Angela continued. "Once we're done there, if we have time, we'll head back to the Lake Mary Loop trail and go for a hike."

Leroy's mouth started to open and Angela silenced him with her hand again. "Rule number three," she said. "When we are not in the bus, you need to stick together and keep your eyes open. Remember what I said about the snakes?"

The kids grew quiet.

"To be safe, you need to do what I say. Got it?"

The girl with the uneven hair looked as if she was about to cry. Ms. Crawford reached forward in her seat, patted the child on the shoulder and smiled reassuringly. "Does everyone understand the rules?"

The children nodded, and then busied themselves practicing using their binoculars. Angela was pleased to see Leroy helping. There seemed to be more good than bad in the boy, provided his energy was channeled correctly.

Angela conducted a head count and came up with fifteen, and then she signaled the driver. The bus lurched forward. "Okay, everyone, you'll want to get your cameras ready if you have them."

Fifteen phones came out of pockets.

About thirty bison waited for them inside the pasture. After everyone had taken pictures and had their questions answered, Angela told the driver to head for E. 72nd and Buckley Road. "Once we get there, I want you to stop about a quarter of mile shy of the intersection." It was off the normal visitors' route, but it would give them the best chance for seeing the burrowing owls.

"Okay, everyone." Angela stood and called for attention, holding onto the bar near the driver as the bus lumbered along the service roads. "We have a huge prairie dog population on the Refuge. They currently take up residence on about 11,000 of our 17,000 acres. We want them to live on about 2,500 acres, so we're working on establishing specific prairie dog towns. We're going to stop at one of the largest designated areas."

"Why don't you guys like prairie dogs?" asked the girl with the braids.

"Because they carry the plague," Leroy answered.

Angela glanced at the boy. "That's not true," she said. "There hasn't been a case of plague found in prairie dogs in the Refuge since 2002."

"My mom says the prairie dogs have fleas that carry communicable diseases."

Ms. Crawford took charge. "Leroy, your mom is worried about something that hasn't happened, yet."

"But she—"

"Please continue, Agent Dimato," Crawford said, placing her hand on his arm and dazzling them all with her smile. The subject was closed.

Angela turned to the girl who had asked the question. "We do like the prairie dogs. But we don't like it when they build tunnels and mounds and eat all the prairie grass, making the land uninhabitable for other wildlife. We're hoping to even things out by reducing the prairie dog population."

The girl frowned. "How do you do that?"

Angela didn't think she should tell her they shoot them or poison them. Instead, she switched gears. "There is one great thing about having lots of prairie dogs. It means we have lots of abandoned prairie dog holes, homes for the burrowing owls."

The girl's face brightened.

"Do any of you know anything about burrowing owls?" Angela asked.

"They're funny to watch," said one of the boys.

Angela nodded. "They are curious birds, active day and night. They love to come out to see who is visiting, so we have a good chance at the site where I'm taking you. What else do you know about burrowing owls?"

"They have really long legs and short tails," said a blond-haired girl.

"That's right," Angela said. "Anything else?" She looked around. "No? Well, unlike most owls, their ears aren't tufted. They kind of look like a mini-football on stilts."

The kids giggled.

"Does anyone know how to tell the male and females apart?"

"The males are bigger," answered one of the boys.

"Good guess, but no," Angela said. "Anyone else?"

"The females feed the babies," said one of the girls.

"You're partially right," Angela said. "The male and female burrowing owls are the same size, but the female spends more time on the nest. That means less time in the sun."

"So the boy birds are suntanned?" Leroy said.

"Sort of. The males' feathers actually get bleached out by the sun, so they look slightly lighter in color. Sometimes," Angela qualified. "Here's a fun fact. Did you know that if you get too near their burrow, the owls can make a sound like a rattlesnake?"

"Are there rattlesnakes out here?" the girl with the uneven haircut asked.

Angela turned to the child. "Yes, but we're not likely to see one. They don't like people, so unless you corner one, they'll usually move on and leave you alone. Does that make you feel any better?"

The girl nodded."

"Great," Angela said. "So, does anyone know what the burrowing owls use to line their nests?"

Everyone, including Crawford and Burton, shook their heads and looked at her expectantly.

"Animal dung," Angela said.

"Poop?" Leroy blurted, punching his seatmate.

"That's right," Angela said. "It keeps the babies warm."

"Gross," said someone, and then chatter among the kids exploded. A few moments later, the bus stopped.

"Now remember," Angela said before letting them off. "You need to be quiet and keep your eyes open. The owls prefer abandoned prairie dog nests, so they can usually be found on the edges of the town."

"I see a prairie dog," shouted a girl.

The kids rushed to her side of the bus, except Leroy. He moved in Angela's direction.

"Inside voices," Ms. Crawford said. She clapped her hands, and the kids quieted down.

"Let's go," Leroy said, pushing past Angela and bounding down the steps. Angela stopped him at the edge of the road. Lifting her binoculars, she scanned the edges of the prairie dog town.

"There." Angela pointed to the far east edge of the town. "If you look straight out, like it's a clock, and back off to the left, you can see some owls at ten o'clock."

The kids trained their binoculars in the direction she pointed.

"I see them," Leroy cried out.

Angela set up the scope for a close up view and let the kids take turns looking at the birds, while she continued scanning the outer edges of the prairie dog town. When she reached the western boundary, two o'clock on her imaginary timepiece, she tightened her focus. It looked like someone kneeling near one of the burrows, straight east of the eagle's roost.

"What the heck?" Angela commandeered the scope. No visitors were allowed in this section of the Refuge, but through the telescopic lens she could clearly see someone about three hundred yards away at the edge of the field.

"What is it?" Leroy asked.

"Stay here," Angela ordered. "I'll be right back."

Leaving Crawford and Burton in charge of the kids, Angela took out across the field. She could feel her adrenalin pumping as she closed in for a confrontation. Whatever this person thought they were doing, they were going to cease and desist immediately.

"Hey, you," she called out.

No response.

As she drew closer, the toe of her boot unearthed a bull snake that slithered away in the dirt. Prairie dogs dove for their holes, while closer to her target several pups popped their heads up to see what was happening.

From fifty yards away, from the way she was dressed, Angela could see it was a woman. She hadn't moved.

"Hey, I'm talking to you."

The woman remained still.

Drawing to within twenty feet, Angela knew why. The woman was positioned with her head on the ground, her knees tucked beneath her, her butt up in the air. Her arms were sprawled to her sides and her face turned sideways, with one eye opened in the blank stare of the dead.

Chapter 2

"Mom!"

Angela turned around and found Leroy Henderson two steps behind her

Leroy bolted forward. Angela caught him around the waist. "Stop!"

"Let me go! That's my mom," he yelled.

Angela turned him away from the scene and held him tight. "You don't know that, Leroy. We have to go back."

Her heart broke for the young boy in her arms. Despite her words, she suspected he would recognize his mother. She remembered how she felt when she had found her partner, Ian, dead. She had known immediately that it was him. There had been nothing anyone could do or say.

Crawford ran toward them through the field. "What is it?"

"You need to go back, Ms. Crawford. Get the kids on the bus. Now!" Angela ordered.

Crawford kept coming across the prairie dog mounds. "Is Leroy hurt? Leroy, are you okay? What happened? Did he get bitten by an animal? A prairie dog? Or a snake?"

"No," Angela said. "Stop and turn around."

"Let me go," Leroy screamed, kicking at Angela's shin. "That's my mom."

Crawford frowned, and then looked past them toward the fence. Shock registered on her face. "Oh my lord, that's Sheila Henderson."

A positive ID. She wanted to ask the teacher when she'd last seen the victim, but didn't because of the boy in her arms.

"Take Leroy." Angela said. "Have the bus driver take you back to the Visitors Center. Wait for me there. Call everyone's parents. We'll send officers to get Leroy's father."

Crawford didn't move. She just stared at the victim.

"Ms. Crawford, did you hear me?" Angela used her free arm to turn the teacher around and push her back toward the road, all the while holding the sobbing boy.

"Yes, yes." Crawford pivoted, and then seemed to rally her senses. "Mr. Burton," she shouted. "Get the children back on the bus." Then she reached for Leroy. "Come with me, honey."

Leroy collapsed into his teacher's arms.

Angela turned and walked the twenty feet to the body. She reached down and felt for a pulse, then pulled out her cell phone. Canon picked up on the third ring. "Wayne, we have a situation in Section 5. I just found a body."

"You what?"

Angela filled him in. "I have no idea what happened. What's the protocol here?"

"Where are the kids?"

"Crawford's getting them back on the bus, and I'm sending them back to the Visitors Center. Apparently, it's the mother of one of the students." She told him about Leroy. She could hear Wayne rustling papers, and waited for him to give her direction.

"The first thing we have to do is notify the DOI that we have a serious incident. We're required to that within fifteen minutes. Has it been that long?"

"Give or take."

"Document the exact time you found her. I'll make the call, and then head out to where you are. Meanwhile, notify the Adams County Sheriff's office and have them send out a team. We're going to treat this like a crime scene. With an unattended death, I'm sure the guys in Washington DC will want a full investigation."

"You'll need to bring out some crime scene tape," Angela said, watching the bus turn around and pull away. Everything she had was back in her truck at the Visitors Center. "What about a victim's advocate?"

"Hold off on that. I'll send Sharon over to the Visitors Center to get everyone's names and start the process of calling parents."

Sharon was Wayne's secretary, a pleasant woman who would be good with the kids. Angela was glad for that. "What about Leroy Henderson's father?"

"Have Adams County send someone over to pick him up."

"Roger that." Angela disconnected, then backtracked to the edge of the road and called Adams County dispatch to get officers on the way. After that, she pulled out her birding notebook and scribbled details of the scene. There wasn't much to note.

Time of discovery: approximately 8:55 a.m.

The victim: a woman.

Blond, approximately 5'7" and one hundred twenty-five pounds, Angela put the woman in her forties. From her position there didn't appear to be any visible signs of trauma, but Angela needed the coroner on scene to move the body. The ground around the body was disturbed, but that could have been caused by a number of things—the victim herself, Angela or any number of animals.

The bigger question was: what was she doing out here? This was a restricted area—no visitors allowed. The perimeter fence to the east was at least a mile away, so the body hadn't been dumped, unless the victim had been alive when she'd been thrown over and had stumbled or crawled to where Angela found her.

Sirens in the distance signaled the sheriff department's arrival. A white patrol car followed by a cloud of dust snaked down 72nd. The vehicle slid to a stop beside Angela and a young deputy jumped out.

"What's the situation?" he asked, starting toward the prairie dog town.

"Hold up," Angela said. "The DOI wants this processed like a crime scene."

"DOI?"

"Department of the Interior. The OLES, Office of Law Enforcement and Security to be exact."

The deputy looked at Angela and narrowed his eyes. "Are you sure she's dead?"

"Yes." Angela squinted at the deputy's name badge. The kid looked fresh out of the academy. "Trust me, Deputy Tanner, I know dead. We need to wait for CSI before we go back out there."

Tanner puffed up his chest. "I think maybe I should check it out, just to be sure, before I call for a crime scene unit."

"If you go out there, you could destroy evidence," Angela said, stepping between the deputy and the field.

A modern Mexican standoff.

Before things could escalate, the cavalry arrived in the form of Wayne Canon.

"Where are the crime scene investigators?" he asked, jumping out of his truck. "OLES wants the scene processed."

"I'm the responding office," Tanner said. "I think I should be the one to make that determination."

"This is federal land," Wayne said. "DOI has jurisdiction. As part of Homeland Security, they're sending out someone from the FBI."

"For a body?" Tanner said.

Wayne stared down the officer. "Until we know what this woman was doing on restricted government property, we will investigate all possibilities. We still have some agents of mass destruction on site."

"I thought they cleaned all that up." Tanner looked a little wild-eyed.

Angela waited to hear Wayne's response. What she considered public knowledge might to him be "need to know."

Wayne cleared his throat. "The Army retains seven hundred twenty-five acres just north of here, with two landfills filled with toxic materials."

Tanner's eyes narrowed. "What type of materials?"

"Are you new around here?" Angela asked.

"Why?"

"This is the old Rocky Mountain Arsenal. They used to make chemical weapons here during World War II."

Tanner's mouth gaped open. "Are you telling me the Army is storing leftover bombs out here?"

"Not that anyone's aware of," Wayne said.

Angela decided now was not the time to point out that the Army had—in 2000, following the discovery of several forty to fifty year-old bomblets filled with Sarin gas—admitted there may be additional bomblets scattered about the Refuge.

"They store everything in capped landfills and monitor them according to EPA standards," Wayne continued. "The DOI just needs assurance that there hasn't been some type of breach."

Tanner jerked his head in the direction of a cluster of warehouse buildings to the west. "Is that Army headquarters?"

"That's the National Eagle and Wildlife Property Repositories," Angela said. "The Army doesn't have an office on the Refuge."

"So what's stored in those buildings?" Tanner asked, still sounding suspicious.

"That's where USFW keeps all the dead eagles, feathers and illegal wildlife trade products that are confiscated."

"Are you talking stuff like ivory?"

"That and stuffed carcasses, jewelry, anything made from protected species," Angela said. "You name it and we've probably got it."

Tanner nodded. Angela figured he was trying to act knowledgeable.

"Hey, here comes CSI," Wayne said.

Tanner looked relieved and gestured to the large white van lumbering up the road, being tailed by an unmarked car. He signaled the van toward the edge of the road. "With any luck, maybe we'll be out of here before the feds show up."

"Too late." Angela said, pointed first to herself and then to Wayne. "We're feds."

Tanner ignored her and turned back to the CSI van. Four techs climbed out. The unmarked car pulled up behind the van and a man in a dark black suit climbed out. He walked toward Wayne and Angela.

"I'm Detective Sykes, Adams County Sheriff's office."

Tanner and Sykes. Angela figured it would pay off to remember the names.

Sykes gazed off across the field, and then pointed to three of the techs. "You three, walk out to the body. Mark anything of interest. You," he instructed the fourth, "take pictures of everything."

"Be careful," Angela instructed. "Some of the mounds may have burrowing owls. They're protected."

After twenty minutes of watching the CSI techs comb the field, Wayne bailed. He put Angela in charge and left explicit instructions for her to call him if anything of interest happened. Twenty-five minutes later, Angela was still leaning against the fender of the patrol car with Tanner and Sykes waiting for an all-clear from the techs. Finally the camera tech signaled and Angela pushed off the fender.

"We're up." Taking out across the field, Angela reached the body first.

"She has no apparent ID," said one of the CSI. "But I can't flip her until the coroner shows."

"Her son and his teacher both identified her as Sheila Henderson," Angela said.

Detective Sykes caught his breath as he squatted beside the body. "Any idea what killed her?"

The camera tech shook his head. "We just process the scene."

The CSIs set up a shade tent to shield the body from the sun and the seven of them waited. A half hour later, the coroner and two assistants showed up followed by two men in suits.

"Sorry we're late," the coroner said. She was a young woman, who—if Angela's memory served—had recently been elected to the position. When Angela didn't ask her to elaborate, she walked over to the body and bent down. "She's dead. Bag her. I'll know more when we can get her on the table in the lab."

"Hold on!" One of the suits flipped open a badge. "FBI. Before you touch the body, we need a recap of what's going on."

Angela brought them up to speed.

"As the USFW agent assigned to the investigation, I'll be coordinating the investigation." She dealt her cards out and then collected five, making sure she had one from all the key players.

"We'll need copies of any and all documentation," said one of the suits.

"Me, too," said Detective Sykes.

"Me three," said Deputy Tanner.

Angela wished she could see everyone's eyes through their sunglasses, and briefly considered putting hers on. She opened her mouth to respond, when a yelp from one of the coroner's assistants caused them all to turn.

"There's a snake." The assistant pointed at a mound near the body.

Deputy Tanner charged forward. "What kind?"

"My guess? A rattlesnake. I only heard it."

Tanner drew his weapon, but Angela blocked his shot.

"Put the gun away," she ordered. "Does anybody have a

shovel?"

"In the van," said one of the CSI, lighting out for the parked vehicles.

Angela waited. If it was a rattlesnake, a shovel was all she needed. She'd try coaxing it back down into the burrow. But if it decided to strike and hit the shovel blade and she would chop off its head.

The tech returned with a short handled spade. Angela took it, stepped around the body and got as close as she could to the mound. Keeping the shovel between herself and the burrow, she moved the blade close to the entrance and heard the warning of the western diamondback.

The coroner's assistants moved farther away, along with three of the CSI techs, the coroner, the two G-men, the detective and the sheriff's deputy. Only Angela, a couple of curious prairie dogs and the camera tech held their ground. The camera tech kept his lens focused on the opening to the burrow.

Angela squatted to get a better look inside the opening. The sun's direction made it hard to see. When she reached for the flashlight on her duty belt, her movement pressed the blade closer to the opening. Again, she heard the rattle.

"It's not backing down," Deputy Tanner said.

"It's not striking either." Angela flicked on her light. "I'm not sure we're dealing with a snake."

The camera tech moved in closer behind her. "What else could it be?"

"Owls," Angela said. "Burrowing owls." She shone her light into the burrow. Six sets of yellow eyes gleamed in the darkness. "They mimic the rattlesnake buzz to deter predators."

The camera tech clicked off a few pictures.

"What's all that crap around the opening?" he asked, reaching forward to pull something free.

"Don't touch that!" Angela ordered. "The owls line their

burrows with dung, and they decorate the entrances with all sorts of objects—feathers, shredded paper, foil and plastic. Mostly they use dried cow and horse dung. It's against federal law to disturb their nests."

The tech snapped a few more pictures, and then the coroner's assistants moved back into position to remove the body. About that time, the two suits and Detective Sykes headed back across the field.

While the assistants bagged the body and loaded it into the wagon, the coroner shook Angela's hand. "We have a pathologist on staff that does the autopsies in-house. I'll mark this one a priority, but it may be a couple of days before I have any preliminary answers. We just came from the scene of a homicide, so there's one ahead of you."

"How long before we can expect an official report?" Angela asked.

"Ten to twelve weeks," said the coroner. "If you're lucky."

Angela nodded. "Do whatever you can."

After the coroner and her assistants departed, they were down to Angela, Deputy Tanner and the CSIs. It didn't take long for the deputy to grow bored.

"I guess I'm not needed around here anymore," he said. "I don't see your truck, Agent. Can I give you a lift somewhere?"

Angela looked at the CSIs bagging evidence.

"We're going to be here a while," the camera tech said.

"My truck is back at the Visitors Center," Angela said. Along with Wayne's secretary, two teachers and a dozen middle-schoolers, unless of course they had all been picked up. "But I need to protect the animals."

"We'll steer clear of the owls," the tech said. "The dung's a great deterrent. My guess is we're going to be here for a couple more hours."

"Okay, then," Angela said. "I'll be back."

Ten minutes later, Tanner pulled up in front of the Visitors Center. En route Angela had learned more about him than she ever wanted to know. He was from the Midwest, he didn't like the grocery store layouts here, he was single and he struggled to make friends. She was glad when he cut the vehicle's engine.

Climbing out of the car, she hurried to the door. It had been around two hours since she'd sent Crawford, Burton and the children back on the bus and the Visitors Center had been closed to the public. Now Wayne's secretary, Sharon, the teachers and Leroy Henderson were the only people inside.

"All the other children were picked up by their parents." Sharon tipped her head in Leroy's direction. "He's the only one left. He asked us to leave him alone."

"What about his father?"

"Wayne called and said two officers went to pick his dad up at his work, but he'd already left. According to the secretary, someone called and said there'd been an emergency and he needed to pick up Leroy. I figure he's on the way."

Angela glanced between the teachers and Leroy. "What about calling a victim's advocate?"

"I did," Sharon said. "But no one's shown up. The boy asked to be left alone."

"Thanks," Angela said. Leroy sat by himself in a chair behind the visitors' information desk, so she walked over and perched on the edge. "How are you doing, kiddo?"

He looked up at her with stricken eyes. "They can't find my dad."

"I'm so sorry."

"He might have taken off," Deputy Tanner said. "Do you think he'd have reason to hurt your mom, kid?"

It was no wonder he didn't have friends.

"Tanner!" Angela admonished.

Leroy's eyes narrowed and he started to tear up.

Angela reached out and touched the boy's shoulder. "Ignore him. He's a butthead."

Leroy looked surprised. "Can you call him that?"

"If the shoe fits," Angela said, glaring at Tanner and daring him to say anything. "Is there anything I can get you, Leroy? Do you feel like a soda?"

The kid shrugged.

"How about a root beer or 7-up? I'm sure Deputy Tanner would love to spring for one. It's the least he can do." *After that bone-headed question.*

Tanner folded his arms across his chest. Angela figured he was trying to look cool.

"You've got to drink something, kid," the deputy said. "What do you want?"

Leroy shrugged again. "A root beer, I guess."

As Tanner headed for the soda machine, Angela called out, "I'll take a Diet Coke."

This time he glared at her over his shoulder.

Angela looked back at Leroy. "Sometimes these guys don't have a clue what they're doing."

Leroy gave her a straight-line grin."

"Seriously though, I do want to ask you a few questions."

Leroy looked down at his hands in his lap and nodded.

"When was the last time you saw your mom?"

"Last night."

"She didn't take you to school this morning?"

Leroy shook his head. "No. My dad did."

Angela made a note to check with Crawford.

"And earlier, you said your mom didn't like prairie dogs."

"She hated 'em."

Angela nodded. "So, do you have any idea what she might have been doing out in the prairie dog town?"

Leroy answered in a virtual whisper. "I heard my dad tell her that, if she was going to be able to do anything about getting rid of the prairie dogs near the soccer fields, she'd have to get proof that they had bad fleas."

Angela considered the possibility that Sheila was trying to collect samples, but she hadn't seen any collection vial.

"Do you know what happened to her?" Leroy asked.

"No," Angela said. "Unfortunately, I don't. But we're going to find out, Leroy. I promise."

"Here you go." Tanner startled her as he came up behind. He handed Leroy a root beer, then Angela a Diet Coke.

As Leroy popped the top on his soda, Crawford called out from in front of the staff office. "Hold on. We don't allow the students to have any sugary drinks."

Angela stood up, ready to do battle, when Burton loomed in the doorway behind her.

"Give the kid a break, Tammy," he said. "We can make an exception here."

Crawford gave a little shake to her head. "You know how it hypes him up."

Just then, a man pounded on the Visitors Center's door.

"It's Mr. Henderson." Burton hurried over to let him in.

Angela took measure of the man entering the lobby. Tall, with a wild shank of light brown hair, he was dressed in blue jeans, work boots and a short-sleeved plaid shirt. His gaze darted around the room until it lit on Leroy.

"What are you accusing my son of doing this time?" he demanded, charging forward across the lobby. "Why are the police here? You can't question him about anything without Sheila or I present. Are you okay, son?"

Leroy's eyes brimmed with tears.

"What have they done to you?"

"Nothing," Angela said, stepping forward. "And Leroy has done nothing wrong."

"Then what the hell is going on? I just got called off a project. My secretary said there was some kind of an emergency."

"Mr. Henderson, would you please sit down?" Angela pointed to a chair near the information desk. "We need to talk to you."

"No, I won't sit down. I want to know what this is about." Henderson was clearly agitated. Again Tanner's hand edged toward his gun.

"It's about your wife, Mr. Henderson," Angela said.

Crawford stepped forward. "We're so sorry," she blurted out.

"Sorry? About what?" Henderson scanned the faces, and then turned back to Angela. He seemed to have lost some of his energy. "What's going on here? Where's Sheila?" He looked at his son. "Leroy?"

The boy started crying and Angela rested her hand on his shoulder again. "Mr. Henderson, I'm sorry to be the one to inform you, but your wife is dead."

Chapter 3

Either Ron Henderson was one heck of an actor or he didn't know anything about what had happened to his wife. It had taken them the better part of an hour to calm him down enough to ask him a few more questions. All he'd been able to verify was that Sheila had said she had an early morning meeting and had asked him to get Leroy up and drop him at school. The last time he had seen Sheila was around five a.m.

It was late afternoon by the time Angela had gotten back to her desk at the Repository. After filling out the paperwork required by the DOI and faxing it to Washington D.C., she had input all of the phone numbers and emails she'd collected into her cell phone and filed the business cards.

Wayne strode into her office as she put the last one away. "So where do we stand on this?"

Angela gave him a recap.

"You know, we need to stay on top of this. OLES isn't going to let this go until we have some answers."

Angela's head hurt. Lacing her fingers through her hair, she closed her eyes and rubbed her temples. "There's nothing more we can do, Wayne. We won't know what happened until we get the coroner's preliminary report."

"Any idea why she was in the prairie dog town?"

"Her husband suggested she was there collecting fleas to try and prove that the prairie dogs carry the plague."

"You're telling me that she left her house early, drove onto the Refuge to cause trouble for us and got herself murdered?"

Angela sighed. "For all we know, she died of natural causes. Until we get the autopsy report, it's all speculation."

"I want to know the minute that report comes in."

His tone carried an urgency that made Angela open her eyes. Wayne started jabbing his finger into the air. "Every single one of the entities that were out there today—the sheriff's department, the coroner's office and the FBI—will be conducting their own investigation. We need to find out what the CSI team uncovers and solve this case, before any of the others do."

Angela lowered her hands to her desk. "Why?"

"What do you mean, why?"

"Why before anyone else?"

"A woman died. It happened on our watch. The DOI is going to be watching how we handle this case."

"It's not like it was our fault, Wayne."

"Easy to say, but you know how bureaucracies are. We don't need any challenge to our jurisdiction or anyone questioning our ability to solve the crime. You need to assert yourself as lead agent. I'd take it on, but I'm in the middle of budgets."

Angela chuckled. "So, that's what this is about. Budgets. You're afraid they're going to cut your funding."

"Let's just say, for the sake of job security, it would behoove you to make sure that the powers that be appreciate the need for law enforcement out here." He moved to the door. "I expect you to get me some answers. *Capiche*?"

Angela thought about how much she enjoyed her job and reached for her keys. "I'm all over it."

She had gone home, taken a shower and fallen asleep the moment her head had hit the pillows. The next morning, heading to work, she detoured by the sheriff's department offices to speak to Detective Sykes.

He was cordial, but showed no interest in the case. Since yesterday morning, he'd been assigned lead on the homicide case that had delayed the coroner the day before. According to

Sykes, Henderson's death sat on a back burner until the coroner deemed it a murder. He recommended Angela follow up with Deputy Tanner.

The rookie wasn't around, so Angela drove to the coroner's office. The receptionist sent her down to the morgue.

Angela pushed open the door to a large room. The walls and floor were covered in white tiles. Stainless steel sinks lined one wall. Body lockers lined another. The staff pathologist stood in the middle of the room. He'd just loaded Sheila Henderson's body onto the slab.

"I'm just getting started. You're welcome to stay."

Angela forced a smile. Autopsies weren't high on her to-do list.

"Thanks," she said, "but maybe I should just leave you to it. What I'm after is the probable cause of death."

"If I were to guess, I'd say she died from an epidural hematoma, a blow to the head. To be exact, a blow to her temple." The pathologist signaled for Angela to move closer. "This was the side of her head facing the ground." He pulled her hair apart and showed Angela the scalp near the temple. "Can you see the marks there? Once I shave her head, I think we'll find patterned bruising. It may give us an idea of the murder weapon. My guess is we'll find massive hemorrhaging on the inside. Look at her eye. See how the pupil on the right is enlarged? And there's clear fluid draining from her ear.

"So you're saying someone hit her?"

The pathologist dropped the clump of victim's hair. "I'm saying she suffered a blow to the head. It's possible someone hit her. It's also possible she suffered a fall and hit her head."

"Except she was half a mile or more away from the nearest trees or fence," Angela said.

"Could she have jumped the fence? It's possible she hit her head on a rock." The coroner moved back toward a small tray with instruments on it.

Angela shook her head. "The burrow where we found her is over a mile away. There's no way she could have gotten over there."

"These types of head injuries are unpredictable. She may have lost consciousness briefly, come around, and even resumed her scheduled activities until experiencing a sudden onset of symptoms."

"How long could she have been fine?"

The pathologist shrugged and reached for a scalpel. "It's hard to say. A person might seem fine for six to eight hours and then suddenly die. Other times, a person will start showing symptoms within minutes, or fall immediately into a coma and never regain consciousness."

The pathologist stepped up to the body, and Angela took a step toward the door.

"So you're saying she could have sustained this head injury as early as midnight the morning she was found?" she asked.

"It's possible. Remember Natasha Richardson?"

"The actress," Angela said.

"That's correct. She suffered a head injury while skiing and checked out fine. It wasn't until an hour or so later that she started showing symptoms—a headache, blurred vision, slurred speech. We call that 'talk and die'-syndrome. But I won't know for sure that's what happened until I get inside her brain."

"Any idea how long her body had been out in that field?"

"Temperatures cool down at night. There were no signs of any predation. I think we could expect that if she'd been out there very long. Best guess, a couple of hours."

As the pathologist pressed the blade to Sheila Henderson's chest, Angela backed out the door. She considered the scenarios. Number one, sometime between midnight and eight-thirty a.m., Henderson hit her head on something. In the morning, she drove out to the Refuge and later died. That would make it an accident. Number two, sometime between those hours, someone hit Henderson on the head. In that case, it didn't matter how long she lived after the fatal blow. It would be murder.

After reaching the parking lot, Angela sat in her truck, rolled down the windows and considered her next move. If Shelia was murdered, the next order of business was to learn more about her. That meant talking to people who knew her. Sheila's husband, Ron, had made it clear that his wife was a stay-at-home mom. According to him, she was, in fact, the de facto leader of the soccer moms. He'd given Angela a few names. At the top of the list was Patricia Litchfield, Sheila's best friend and confidant. Angela would start there.

* * *

The Litchfield's lived two houses down from the Henderson's, in an upper middle-class neighborhood on the north side of the Refuge, in one of the newer housing developments. Large, multi-level houses in shades of tan and blue were packed in tightly side-by-side, on wide streets that curved through the development. Each house had a two-car garage, and a square of grass with trees planted near the sidewalks and fenced backyards. She guessed the median income of the residents in this development was encroaching on three figures.

Passing the Henderson's house, Angela took note of the drawn shades and the paper still on the front stoop. She pictured the father and son inside, sitting and staring at the walls, both paralyzed with grief. Based on her observations of the day before, she couldn't imagine how the two of them were going to survive.

Parking on the street in front of the Litchfield's home, Angela walked up the driveway, onto the front walk, then climbed the steps to the porch and knocked. The door was answered by a woman wearing a terrycloth bathrobe. Her dark hair was clipped up in a rat's nest of curls. Puffy, red eyes showed she'd been crying.

"Patricia Litchfield?"

"Yes?"

"I'm Agent Angela Dimato with U.S. Fish and Wildlife. I'm investigating Shelia Henderson's death. Do you mind if I ask you a few questions?"

"This is really not a good time," Litchfield said.

It was never a good time. "I understand," Angela said. "But it won't take long. It's important."

Litchfield hesitated, then stepped back from the door and headed into the bowels of the house. "Close the door behind you, please."

Angela shut the door and followed the woman past a large open living room area and a dining room, and into a bright, airy kitchen. A breakfast nook looked out into a postage stamp-sized back yard surrounded by a six foot high security fence.

"Would you like a cup of coffee?" Litchfield said, waving toward a seat at the table.

Angela pulled out a chair. "Only if it's already made."

A few minutes later, with two steaming mugs of coffee in hand, Litchfield joined her at the table. "What do you want to know?"

"I realize this is hard, Mrs. Litchfield."

"Patty. I go by Patty."

Angela nodded. "I'm trying to figure out why Sheila Henderson was inside the Refuge, crawling around near a burrow of owls."

"She wouldn't have hurt them, if that's what you think. She loved birds."

Angela sipped her coffee. "Maybe, but her son told me that she didn't much like the prairie dogs."

Patty Litchfield set her mug down hard, sloshing coffee over the sides. "Who does? They're nasty little creatures that leave holes all over the soccer fields. And you, of all people, must know that the dirty rodents carry bubonic plague. Four Adam's County residents have died this year."

Angela was aware of the deaths and none of them were connected to the prairie dogs on or near the Refuge. In all four cases, the victims had come in contact with plague-positive fleas carried on rats living in their home.

"Do you think Sheila was in the Refuge trying to collect evidence of the disease?"

"I suppose it's possible, but that doesn't really sound like Sheila. All she really wanted was for the city to put up a special barrier, to contain the prairie dogs and keep them off the school grounds."

"What kind of barrier?"

"Some type of visual barrier." Patty pushed her hair back. "Sheila read about it in some engineering magazine of Ron's. The article claimed that if you hung some sort of blackout tarping low on a fence, it would block the prairie dogs ability to see beyond it and make them hesitant to cross the barrier. It's expensive, but completely humane. She was against the normal types of control, like shooting or poisoning the animals. She said that killed the birds and, like I said, Sheila liked birds."

Angela watched tears well up and then spill from Patty's eyes. The woman reached for a tissue.

"So Sheila appealed to the city to fund this fence?" Angela said.

"That's right." Patty dabbed at her tears. "She originally petitioned the school, but the school board wouldn't consider it. It was after that Sheila approached the city council for money.

They refused, too, but she was prepared. She filed a lawsuit against the school district, and she would have won. She knew her way around the system."

"How so?"

Patty shrugged. "Before she and Ron got married, Sheila was a legal secretary. She was never afraid to fight for what she believed in. She decided if the school board and city council didn't want to build us a fence, she would force the issue."

"By doing what?"

"Sheila filed a lawsuit over the conditions on the soccer field. We have kids from kindergarten to high school that play ball on the field, and several kids have been hurt running into a prairie dog mound. And it's only a matter of time before someone catches the plague."

"Did she file this suit on behalf of the soccer league?"

Patty shook her head. "The soccer league didn't want anything to do with it, but most of the soccer moms are behind her. It's our kids that are getting hurt out there."

"So she filed on behalf of herself?"

"No, she filed on Leroy's behalf. Last year he stepped in a hole and broke his ankle. Sheila filed a one million dollar lawsuit against the school district for medical bills, pain and suffering."

"What happened?" Angela asked.

Patty leaned forward. "The school suspended the soccer program for the upcoming year, pending the outcome. It made some of the parents mad. One father in particular. He threatened her. He said she'd be sorry if she didn't drop the lawsuit."

Angela could see how shutting down a major recreational program would have the potential to make people angry. She dug her notebook out her pocket. "What was the man's name?"

Patty sat back. "Oh, he didn't really mean it. He was just mad, you know?"

"I'd still like to talk to him." Angela found a pen and looked up at Patty. The woman looked away, twisting the tissue in her hand.

"You have to understand," Patty said. "His son is a senior this year. The family was counting on a soccer scholarship for him to go to college. He would have been the first one in his family. I've never seen Ron so mad."

"Sheila's husband? You can't really blame him," Angela said. "The man threatened his wife."

"Oh, Ron wasn't mad at Ken. He was furious with Sheila. He claimed it made Leroy a target for bullies. As if anything or anyone could scare that kid." Patty shook her head. "Of course, they'd been having some problems."

"Ron and Sheila?" Angela asked. That was a new twist.

Patty nodded. "Sheila told me she thought Ron was having an affair."

"With who?"

Patty suddenly stood and shoved back her chair.

"I think I've said too much," she said, picking up her mug and walking over to the kitchen sink. "I think I'd like you to leave now."

That was her cue. Angela stood and carried her own mug to the sink. "Look, your friend is dead. I know you want to help me find out what happened to her. I really need those names."

Patty looked up from the sink. Angela tried to smile encouragingly. She could see the doubt flicker through the woman's eyes.

"Ken Martinez," she finally said. "That's the name of the man who threatened Sheila."

"And the woman she thought was having an affair with her husband?"

Patty looked back at the sink and started rinsing the mugs. Angela waited. When she finally spoke, her voice was barely a whisper.

"Ellie. Ellie Parker."

"Thank you." Angela considered reaching out and touching Patty's back, but then thought better of it. Comfort wasn't her strong suit. "I can let myself out. Thanks for the coffee."

Patty's head dipped.

Angela was halfway to the door when she thought of one last question and turned around. "You said Sheila loved birds."

"So?" Patty said, stepping into the kitchen doorway.

"Did she ever go birding on the Refuge?"

"She went there all the time." Patty snickered. "That used to make Ron mad, too. Her favorite place to go was over by the eagle's roost."

First Creek was off-limits to self-guided visitors. "I take it she drove over there."

"Of course, it's too far to walk." Patty stuffed her hands in the pockets of her robe and wrapped it tightly around her. "Sheila took me there once to see the bald eagles."

Angela made another mental note—to look near the roost for Sheila Henderson's car. After taking Leroy home yesterday afternoon, Ron had reported it missing. Deputy Tanner had issued an all-points-bulletin and it hadn't been found, yet. The car wasn't on the Refuge. At least, not in any of the obvious places—the Visitors Center parking lot or anywhere near where Sheila's body was found. It was a half-mile hike from the eagle's roost to the prairie dog town, but doable, especially if she wanted to hide her vehicle for some reason. Though what that reason could be, Angela had yet to fathom.

Chapter 4

It took ten minutes for Angela to get from Patty Litchfield's house to the National Eagle Repository building. When she arrived, she found a message from the coroner's office on her desk. The news was bad. The pathologist confirmed that Sheila Henderson had died from blunt force trauma to her temple. Based on the bruising pattern, it appeared she'd been struck with some type of round object that caused massive internal bleeding. The only other oddity was a sticky residue on her hand they hadn't been able to identify.

"What's new?"

At the sound of Wayne's voice in the doorway, Angela looked up from the slip of paper in her hand. "The coroner just ruled it a homicide."

"*Damn*! We'll have to inform the OLES."

"Of course <u>you will</u>," Angela said, trying not to sound too sarcastic over his use of the proverbial "we." She told him about her conversation with Patty Litchfield.

"Maybe we should take a ride out to First Creek," Wayne said. "Give me fifteen minutes to file the report with DOI and I'll meet you out front."

"No problem." Angela marked the time, and then sat down at her desk and booted up her computer. She had three known people of interest—Ron Henderson, Ken Martinez and Ellie Parker—and a quarter hour to burn.

Accessing the law enforcement database, she looked up all three names. Ken Martinez was the only one with a record. Ten years ago, he'd spent one night in jail for an assault at a local bar. All charges had been dropped the next day.

A Google search proved more fruitful.

Ron Henderson had a Linked-In page. His resume listed him as a civil engineer for the Colorado Department of Transportation out of District 1. He had taken a job with CDOT straight out of college, started as an engineer-in-training in District 2 and moved up the ranks. He was now the Resident Engineer of District 1, overseeing road and bridge operations.

Ken Martinez didn't have a Linked-In page, but based on random articles in the *Commerce City Sentinel*, it appeared his biggest claim to fame was being the father of soccer superstar, Ken Jr. One write up listed his profession as shift supervisor at the local Walmart. He also had a daughter, who was a junior at Adam's City High School.

A Department of Motor Vehicle search turned up an Elizabeth Parker living in Commerce City. Angela searched the property database and found her owning a residence with Samuel Bernel Parker in the Reunion area north of the Refuge.

Wayne waited impatiently beside his USFW truck by the time Angela left the building. "I thought I was going to have to come up and get you. Get in."

Climbing up into the passenger seat, she rolled down the window and enjoyed the breeze as he headed out 72nd and pulled onto the Caps and Covers Road. It was a beautiful day. In the distance she could see the Denver skyline rising against the backdrop of the Continental Divide. A hawk spun lazy circles in the sky overhead and a small herd of white-tailed deer frolicked in the trees along the edge of Lower Derby Lake. Rejoining 72nd, Wayne drove like they were headed to the crime scene except instead of heading straight, he turned south on what remained of Chambers Road.

A chain with the "Closed to the Public" sign crossed the road, and Angela got out and opened the gate. From there the service road was a track, two gravel strips with grass growing in the center, rutted and washed out from last year's floods. She kept her eyes open for any sign of a vehicle parked off the road.

"I don't see how she could have got in here without someone seeing her," Wayne said, wrestling with the steering wheel of the truck. "What kind of car does she drive?"

"A 4-Runner," Angela said. "Gray."

Just before the narrow bridge that marked the north end of the eagle's roost, Wayne pulled off into a small turnaround area. He parked the truck on the shortgrass under a large cottonwood tree. Angela climbed out and studied the tracks in the turnaround.

"I don't see any useable tire marks or footprints, but its clear several people have been out here recently."

"Don't disturb anything," Wayne said. "DOI will want CSI to confirm."

Angela bristled. She knew the protocol and didn't appreciate him pointing out the obvious. "We don't even know for sure that she was the one who was out here."

"Who else could it have been?" he said, fumbling in his pocket for his phone. "She's the only one dead with a missing car who's BFF said she loved birds."

While he called dispatch, Angela circled the area. On the west side of the clearing, she made a gruesome discovery—an eagle feather with a bloody quill.

Wayne punched off his phone. "Adam's County is sending a unit, along with Deputy Tanner." He jerked his head in her direction. "What do you have there?"

"A feather." Angela held it up. "It looks like it's been plucked from a bird."

"So she wasn't just collecting," Wayne said. "She was taking."

"An actionable offense," Angela said. The Bald Eagle Protection Act of 1940 made it illegal for anyone to "take, possess, sell, purchase, barter, offer to sell, transport, export or import, at any time or in any manner, any bald eagle commonly known as the American eagle, alive or dead, or any part, nest, or egg thereof of." The Act was amended in 1972 to include golden eagles, but the basics were clear—you couldn't pick a feather up off the ground without facing charges.

A first violation could result in a $5,000 fine and imprisonment for one year. A second offense doubled the penalty.

Noting the blood and skin around the base of the quill, this feather was recently pulled from the body of a bird. Whoever had done this deserved to have the book thrown at them.

Angela squatted down, looked at the ground. "It looks like it happened recently."

"Maybe she came down here looking for feathers and got caught," Wayne said.

Angela straightened up. "If that's the case, why clock her in the head and then leave the feather behind? And, if they knew the value of the feather, why not turn her in for the reward?" According to the Act, anyone with information leading to a conviction received half of the fine assessed. Using Wayne's logic, if someone had caught her with an eagle feather, Sheila would have been the one with the motive for murder.

"I see your point." Wayne rubbed his hand across his mouth and scrunched up his face in thought. "Maybe she caught someone else in the act?"

That actually made more sense to Angela, but then where was the rest of the bird? Plucking feathers out of a cold carcass was hard work, and no one was going to yank a feather out of a live bird.

"I wonder where her car is?" she wondered out loud. Finding it might fill in more of the gaps. "The victim had to get out here somehow."

"That's what I'm paying you to find out," Wayne said, heading back toward his truck. "Meanwhile, I'm going back out to the road to wait for the deputy and CSI."

"I'll keep looking around here," Angela said. Not that it mattered. He was already gone.

Canvasing a wider area, she turned up a spot on the edge of the turnaround where a scuffle might have taken place. There were more than the usual amounts of broken branches, though the disturbance could have been caused by the deer that lived in the area.

She walked back to the bridge and crossed, walking along the west bank of First Creek toward the area where she knew the eyrie to be. Finding no more signs of people, she stopped after a few hundred feet and took in the beauty. On the east side of the creek, running north and south, ran a line of large cottonwoods where the bald eagles shared a communal roost high in the trees in January and February. Currently, one tree at the southern end housed a nesting pair and their two fledglings.

A loud whistle signaled Wayne's return and Angela turned back. In the minutes it took her to return to the turnaround, the techs were building molds to make casts of the tire impressions.

"Want to take a walk out to the nest, Wayne?" Angela asked. "The feather I found wasn't molted, which means someone pulled it out of a bird."

Leaving Deputy Tanner to supervise the casts, Wayne and Angela grabbed their binoculars and hiked back north along the road. They crossed the bridge, then cut straight east into the field on a beeline for the spot where Shelia Henderson's body was found. When they reached the far side of the trees, they cut back south toward the nesting tree.

Wayne and Angela walked along slowly, looking for signs of disturbance. Shuffling marks on the ground gave clear signs that they weren't the only recent visitors. Angela used her phone and snapped a couple of photos.

"None of these will be of any use," Wayne said.

Angela had drawn the same conclusion. "I just hope we don't find that the nest has been disturbed."

Her gut was telling her different. Selling eagle parts was lucrative. Wing feathers sold for as much as $150 a piece and tail feathers for $250. An eagle had twelve tail feathers, twenty primary wing feathers and twenty-eight secondary wing feathers. Add in the other items of value, like the talons and beak, a full bird could net upwards of $10,000.

She also knew it wasn't hard to find a buyer. The black market demand was huge. Private collectors paid thousands for Native American memorabilia, and there were a growing number of non-Indians embracing Native American beliefs and ceremonies. Even among the Native Americans the demand had increased. Any tribal members could request parts from the National Eagle Repository, but the wait-time was as long as two years for parts from a bald eagle and five years for parts from a golden eagle.

Reaching the tree with the eyrie, Angela backed deep into the field and trained her binoculars upward. The nest still rested near the top of the tree. Six or seven feet across and two feet deep, it appeared to be intact—a jumbled mass of sticks and twigs.

A shadow crossed the nest and Angela looked up. An adult bald eagle swept in, a large northern pike dangling from its talons. As if on cue, the two eaglets appeared, jumping up on the edge of the nest and screaming for food.

The adult eagle flew past, then circled back, staying just out of reach as if daring its youngsters to fly.

The eaglets strutted back and forth, their mouths open, demanding to be fed. Mostly brown, their wings and bodies were mottled with varying shades of white. At this stage, both of the parents spent most of their time hunting for food and the eaglets spent most of their time alone in the nest.

Angela let herself relax. So far, everything appeared to be fine. Looping her binoculars around her neck, she signaled to Wayne.

"What?" he said.

"Let's check the crime scene."

Together they moved toward the ring of yellow tape flapping at the edge of the prairie dog town. The wind blew errant strands of hair from her ponytail into her face, and Angela turned her face into the steady breeze. The sun beat down. With nothing else to go on, the next step was finding Sheila Henderson's car. With any luck, they'd missed something at the crime scene.

Chapter 5

The yellow and black tape encircled a large section of the prairie dog town, stretching one-thousand feet from the location of the body in every direction. The two-track path still referred to as E. 72nd Ave. served as the northern perimeter. In half a mile, it intersected with a service road running parallel to Buckley Rd. To the south and west there were just more prairie dogs.

"Let's check the fence," Angela said, heading east along the road, though she didn't believe Sheila Henderson had across that way.

At the gravel service road, they turned south and walked along the ten foot chicken-wire fence that separated Buckley from the Refuge. On the outside of the barrier, there were places where people had pulled in and parked. But, based on the scattered beer cans and cigarette butts, Angela figured the litter came from high school kids out on a Saturday night. She and Wayne found no signs that anyone had been on the ground inside the fence.

After walking about a thousand feet, Wayne started to turn back.

"Wait," Angela said. "Let's go as far as the eagle watch."

"What for?"

"Maybe Sheila saw something from out there."

"It's hot. I say we go back and get my truck. It has air conditioning."

"Whimp." Angela continued to head south, figuring Wayne would either follow or go back and then drive around and pick her up.

"Let's at least save ourselves some time," he said, striking out across the prairie dog field. Prairie dogs scattered in all directions, some diving for their holes, some rising up in their holes and barking from a safe distance.

"What the hell are you doing?" Angela asked. The policy was to avoid walking through the prairie dog towns, especially in the summer when the burrowing owls were nesting.

"I'm cutting a half-mile off our hike."

Angela hesitated, and then followed him. There were no burrowing owls here. This was the heart of the prairie dog town, with mounds spreading out in all directions for a half-mile or more. The worst harm they might do is cave in a mound and twist an ankle.

At the eagle watch, they both stood on the wooden platform and scanned the area with their binoculars. There were signs that people had driven out here in the past few days, but who? Sheila?

"What if she saw someone out near the eyrie?" Angela said. "She might have decided to go over and tell them to leave the area. According to her BFF she was very protective of the eagles."

"Alone?"

Angela shrugged. It wouldn't have stopped her, but then she carried a gun. "Okay, so maybe she got in her car and headed for the repository offices to find a ranger."

"Or maybe she just drove away."

He had a point. There were only two ways out—south or north, and then west. Most visitors would have headed back south to E. 64th St. and then to the Visitor's Center. While the road was closed to sightseers past the Wildlife Drive turn-around, the lower route was better maintained for those days the eagle watch was opened.

The other route was taking E. 72nd Ave., the two-track road they had just walked. It was off limits to all visitors east of C St.

The entire way Sheila would have been on unmaintained roads. She would have driven right past the mouth of First Creek, and then been forced to wind around on the Caps and Covers Road to the USFW Law Enforcement offices. Most people wouldn't have chosen that route, but—according to Patty Litchfield—Sheila was very familiar with Rocky Mountain Arsenal property.

"Let's say she saw something she wanted to report," Angela said. "Maybe she left here in a hurry, or was being followed, and then crashed her car. If it happened on 64th, someone would have spotted her vehicle by now. But there are several places along 72nd and Caps and Covers where a car might remain hidden for months."

"Maybe years," Wayne said. "Nobody drives these roads."

They cut back through the fields going straight west, then back north along the boundary of the crime scene. Angela kept her eyes open for signs that anyone had been walking out in the field. Except for the damage Wayne caused by scuffling his feet on the dry ground, there were no signs of any human incursion. The land had been scrubbed free by the constant winds that swept across the prairies.

At the juncture of 72nd and Chambers, Wayne again lobbied to go and pick up the truck. Angela pressed on another four-hundred feet to an area where willows, skunkbrush and cottonwoods pressed in along the banks.

"Do you see any signs of a vehicle leaving the path?" she asked.

"It looks like a car might have turned around here," Wayne said, pointing to some tracks on the side of the road.

Angela kept walking. After another two-hundred feet she was about to give up, when she spotted a flash of gray deep in the vegetation.

"There," she said, pushing her way through the thicket. Nearly hidden in the skunkbrush she found Shelia Henderson's car. The gray 4-Runner had veered off the road and plowed into a dense tangle.

"You were right," Wayne said. "Now all we have to do is figure out why she lost control of her car."

Angela backed away from the car. Regardless of why Sheila had crashed into the bushes, the car might yield a clue as to what had happened to her. From the dirt on the mats, the CSI might be able to determine whether or not she had been down near the eagles' nest. Fingerprints might place someone else at the scene. A re-creation of the accident might determine whether or not she had sustained the head injury in the crash. Maybe this <u>was</u> just an accident. "Talk and die"-syndrome could account for her body turning up three-quarters of mile away from the site of the wreck face-first in a prairie dog hole. If she'd been disoriented, she could have gotten turned around and walked in the wrong direction.

It took two hours for the car to be towed, and a preliminary examination of the vehicle didn't turn up any evidence tying Sheila with the eagle feather. The coroner stood behind his conviction that she had died from a blow to the head by a foreign object with specific patterning. The steering wheel wasn't a match. Also according to the report, the blow had been struck sometime between midnight and eight a.m. It was time to find out where she was during those hours.

Angela's first stop was the Henderson's house off of E. 96th Street. The shades were still drawn, and another paper had been added to the stoop. It didn't look like anyone had come in or out in two days.

Stepping over the papers, she knocked on the front door. It opened to the length of the chain and Leroy stuck his nose out.

"What do you want?"

"I want to talk to your dad."

"He isn't here."

Angela frowned. Technically, in the state of Colorado, a child could be left home alone for short periods of time once they reached twelve years of age. As a middle-schooler, Leroy would qualify, though under the circumstances leaving him alone seemed callous if not irresponsible. "When's he coming back?"

"He went to the store."

"How about I visit with you until he gets back?"

"I'm not supposed to let anyone in."

Good instructions, thought Angela. Through the crack in the door, she could see that the house was a mess. From the blankets on the couch, the glasses on the coffee table and crumbled bags of chips on the floor, it looked like one or both of them had been camping in the living room the last couple of days.

"What if we sat out here, on the front porch?"

Leroy shut the door in her face, and Angela wasn't sure if that meant no or if he intended to unchain the door. She waited a couple of minutes and considered knocking again, when he opened the door. He came out onto the porch wearing the same clothes he'd worn on the fieldtrip. Walking past her, he sat down on the top step.

"How are you doing, Leroy?" she asked, sitting down beside him. She wasn't quite sure how to approach him. But when she was a kid, the thing she had hated the most was when people had talked down to her. She figured her best chance at having a dialogue with Leroy was to treat him like a little adult.

He shrugged.

"It's got to be hard. Is it just you and your dad here? Do you have any family coming?"

"My aunt, my mom's sister, is coming this afternoon."

That was good, she hoped. Sometimes family was the last thing you needed. "How's your dad doing?"

"Not great." Leroy looked at her pointedly. "What do you want to ask my dad about? You're not going to accuse him of doing something to my mom again?"

Angela shook her head. "No. I just need to know where your mom was starting at around midnight last night."

"For a timeline," Leroy said.

Angela scrunched up her nose. "It sounds like you watch a lot of crime television."

Leroy nodded. "The first thing the cops do is figure out where someone was right before he dies, so they can figure out when he was killed and who killed him."

"You'd make a good detective."

Leroy shook his head, bent forward and picked a small pebble up off the step, and pitched it into the grass. "I want to be an astronaut."

"Or that," Angela said. She needed to press. "So, was your mom here all night?"

"No." Leroy looked up. "I bet you were hoping I'd say yes, weren't you?"

"That would've made my life easier."

Leroy looked back at the step. "She and my dad were both gone. My dad went out with some of the guys from his work, and my mom said she had something to do, so she called Jessy."

Angela took it that "Jessy" was the babysitter. "Does Jessy have a last name?"

Leroy shrugged again. It seemed to be his favorite gesture

"Do you remember what time either of your parents came home?"

"No. Jessy made me go to bed." Leroy pitched another pebble. "That's all I know until my dad woke me up. By then my mom was already gone."

Chapter 6

Angela sat with Leroy until Ron Henderson came home. When he pulled up, he got out, grabbed a handful of grocery bags and charged the steps.

"What are you doing here?" he demanded.

"I came to talk to you."

"This isn't a good time."

Angela ignored him. "Any chance we could talk alone?"

Ron looked between her and Leroy, and then blew out a breath. "Leroy, take these inside."

Angela stood and waited for Leroy to disappear into the house.

"We found your wife's car," she said.

"Where?"

"About a half-mile from where we found her body. It's been towed to the impound lot. Once the crime scene investigators are through going over it, someone will call you."

"And make me pay to bail it out."

Unfortunately, that was how it worked. Angela didn't think it was fair, but the county had to cover its costs somehow.

Instead of answering, she said, "Leroy tells me you were out last night."

"Yeah, so?"

"Mr. Henderson, according to the coroner's preliminary report, your wife died from a blow to the head, a blow that could have been sustained any time after midnight. Do you know if she had any sort of accident or altercation with someone?"

"No."

His answer came too quickly, so Angela waited.

Henderson ran his hands through his hair and blew out another breath. "Look," he said. "Sheila and I were having some problems. Don't get me wrong, I loved my wife, but..."

Angela tried to look sympathetic. "Her friend, Patty, told me she thought you were seeing someone."

A flash of panic crossed Henderson's face and he turned toward his car. Angela followed him down the steps.

"She says you were seeing one of your co-workers. Is that true?"

"No." He looked Angela square in the eyes. "Last night, I was out with colleagues. Shelia was pissed. She said if I was going out, so was she. She hired a babysitter. She was still out when I got home. She must have come home late and slept in the guest room, because I didn't see her until she was leaving at five a.m."

"I need the name of the bar, and a list of your colleagues who were there," Angela said.

Henderson narrowed his eyes. "Blame the husband. That's what cops always do. Well, I didn't kill my wife."

That's what they always said. "It's routine, Mr. Henderson. My job requires that I document your wife's final hours, which means accounting for the people she lives with."

"Garcia's. I was there until just before closing."

Angela wrote down the name. For some reason, it rang a bell. "And the names of the people you were with?"

"No. I'm not dragging anybody else into this." Henderson picked up the last of the grocery bags in the car and slammed the door. "Are we done?"

"Just one last question, what's the name of your babysitter?"

"Jessy Martinez."

The name sounded familiar. "Ken Martinez's daughter?"

"The same, only she lives with her mother about two blocks over."

"Thanks, Mr. Henderson. We'll be in touch about the car. I'm really sorry for your loss." It sounded condescending.

She watched him stomp up his front walk, and then she climbed into her truck. The next step was obvious. She needed to talk to Jessy

A quick search turned up an address for Maria Martinez, two blocks over. Angela decided to make a cold call at the residence and turned the key in the ignition. En route she phoned Deputy Tanner and asked him to arrange for a talk with Ken Martinez. She told him she needed forty-five minutes and to text her specifics.

The houses on the block where Jessy lived looked just like the houses on the block where Patty Litchfield and the Henderson's lived—blue or tan, multi-level with two car garages, front steps, small porches. Climbing the steps to ring the doorbell, she noticed a beat up Chevy parked in the driveway. Someone appeared to be home.

Angela rang the doorbell and waited. When no one responded, she rang the doorbell again and banged the front door knocker.

"Coming," someone yelled. Angela heard pounding on the stairs and then the door opened to reveal a teenage girl with an unruly mop of dark hair twisted up in a ponytail.

"Who is it, darling?" called a woman from upstairs.

"I don't know," the girl shouted back. "Who are you?"

"Agent Angela Dimato. U.S. Fish and Wildlife."

The girl looked confused, and then the realization struck. "You're here about Mrs. Henderson's murder, aren't you? That's so sad."

"I'm here about her death. It's still under investigation."

A woman wearing blue jeans and a t-shirt, and who looked like an older version of Jessy, came down the stairs. "What's this about?"

Angela introduced herself again. "I just need to ask Jessy a couple of questions."

"Like what?" the older woman asked.

"Mom, it's fine," Jessy said. "Shoot."

"When was the last time you saw Mrs. Henderson?"

"Just after I got there. She called and asked if I could watch the monster for a couple of hours. I said, sure. I can always use the money."

"So you weren't there when she got back home?"

"Nah, Mr. Henderson came in around two-thirty a.m. He paid me and let me go home."

"I told her when she left that I didn't want her staying out past one a.m.," Maria Martinez said. "That's plenty late for a young girl to babysit."

"Mom, just leave it."

Clearly mother and daughter didn't see eye-to-eye. "Did she tell you where she was going?" Angela asked.

"Nah, well, wait. She said she was going to meet Mr. Henderson somewhere. I was kind of surprised when he came home without her, but it's none of my business."

"They're usually pretty good about getting back on time," Maria said. "It surprised me that they kept Jessy so late."

From the expression on Jessy's face, Angela figured the girl never told them about her curfew. "Thanks."

"Sure thing." Jessy nodded and bounded away.

Maria nodded and started to close the door, when Angela thought to ask her about her ex. "One more thing."

"Yes?" Maria seemed wary.

"What can you tell me about the relationship between Sheila Henderson and your ex-husband? I hear they'd had a falling out."

"That woman may have cost our Kenny a scholarship opportunity. He is a star soccer player, and now the school district has suspended all play because of her stupid lawsuit. They won't let the kids on the field until there's a ruling in the case and some decision has been made about how to repair the soccer fields. If Kenny can't play, who will recruit him?"

"And that made your husband mad."

"It made me mad, too. It made a lot of us mad."

"But according to at least one person, your husband threatened her."

"He said she would be sorry. It's what people say when they're mad."

Angela had to admit, she'd be rich if she had a nickel for every time her own father had said, "I just want to kill you," and didn't mean it.

"Do you think Ken would've hurt her? He does have a record for violence."

Maria stepped outside and pulled the door shut. "That happened a long time ago," she said, her voice low. "Ken was barely twenty-one. Some guy was hitting on me in the bar and got a little physical, if you know what I mean. Ken punched him and broke the guy's nose. The guy had it coming."

"Sounds like it," Angela said. Defending his wife, or future wife's honor, was a far cry from someone who was prone to violence. "Just one more question. Why, if there's bad blood between your families, did you let Jessy babysit for the Henderson's?"

"What's going on is between Ken and Sheila," Maria said, pushing open the door. "Why should Jessy pay the price for that?"

Angela thanked Maria again and went back to the truck. Checking her phone, she found a text from Tanner. He'd arranged to meet Ken Martinez at his house at six p.m., after he finished his shift. That gave her just over an hour to grab something to eat.

The neighborhood Ken Martinez lived in was shabby in contrast to his ex-wife's neighborhood. Here the houses were ranch-style, smaller and packed more tightly together. Kids rode their bicycles up and down the streets. Families were out in their yards. It reminded Angela of the neighborhood she'd grown up in, where everyone knew your business.

Deputy Tanner was parked at the curb, and climbed out of his vehicle when Angela pulled up behind.

"He's home," Tanner said. "He pulled into his drive about five minutes ago, and he knows we're out here."

"We made an appointment, and we're not here to arrest him," Angela said, leading the way up the paving stones that cut through a postage-stamp sized yard. "We're just going to ask him a few questions."

"Gotcha."

Martinez opened his front door before Angela and Tanner reached the end of the walk.

"What's this about?" Martinez asked, blocking their entry.

"Shelia Henderson."

"What's that bitch up to now?"

"She's dead," Tanner said.

Angela watched the color leave Martinez's face. The man hadn't known. "She was found dead yesterday morning," she said. "We hear you had some trouble with her."

"Who didn't?" Martinez said. "Come on in. We can go out in the back." He led the way through a small, neat house to a small, neatly trimmed backyard. Angela noticed a bird feeder hanging from the limb of the large cottonwood that shaded the grass. Small gray birds swamped the feeder and decorated the branches of the shrubbery, keeping a determined red squirrel at bay. Four chairs lined a concrete patio. He gestured for them to sit down.

"Mr. Martinez, when was the last time you saw Sheila Henderson?" Angela asked.

"A week or two ago. We weren't friends."

"People say you threatened her," Tanner said.

Martinez looked at the deputy. "I didn't hurt her, if that's what you think. She made trouble for my boy. She made trouble for a lot of people."

"Because of the soccer program?" Angela asked.

"Because of a lot of things. That woman liked to sue people. She was always looking for an angle to get what she wanted."

Angela took out her notebook. "Besides you, who else was she suing?"

"Who hadn't she sued might be a better question. She sued her homeowner's association for allowing one of her neighbors to paint their house an unauthorized shade of blue. She sued her landscape architect for planting trees in her yard that died. She sued some kid for rear-ending her car and wanted his insurance company to pay her a million dollars. The woman was a sleazy lawyer's wet dream."

"So you admit she was a nuisance that you'd just as soon be rid of?" Tanner said. Angela wanted to kill him.

"She was a pain alright, but that doesn't mean I did anything to her." Martinez looked at Angela. "Do I need a lawyer?"

"Deputy Tanner isn't accusing you of doing anything, Mr. Martinez," Angela said.

Tanner shrugged, as if to say maybe he was, maybe he wasn't.

Martinez focused on Angela. "What time did you say she was murdered?"

"We didn't," Tanner said. "How do you know she was murdered?"

Martinez glared at the deputy. "Why else would you come here asking questions?"

"Mr. Martinez, where were you two nights ago?" Angela asked.

"Work," he answered. "I worked a double shift. The night shift super called in, so I was at work from eleven until eight a.m. You can verify with the general manager."

"We'll do that," Tanner said.

"Mr. Martinez, do you know the names of anyone else who might want to harm Sheila Henderson?" Angela asked.

"You might want to talk to her husband."

"Why's that?"

"Those two were not getting along. Sheila told everyone who would listen that she thought he was having an affair. I think she was hoping someone would confirm her suspicions and give her a name." Martinez pushed out of his chair. "Are we about finished? I haven't eaten yet, and I haven't slept much for a couple of days. I'd like to get myself dinner and hit the hay."

Martinez showed Angela and the deputy out.

Angela kept her mouth shut until they were seated inside Tanner's patrol car, then she turned on the deputy. "What the heck was that, Tanner? We were here asking questions, not here to accuse him of anything. He might have given us more answers if you'd been more civil."

"He has motive," the deputy said. "I was trying to smoke him out."

"You almost forced him to lawyer up."

"I figured maybe if I pushed him a little he would tip his hand."

"From my experience, you push and people clam up," Angela said. "Next time, can we try it my way?"

Tanner shrugged.

Angela wanted to shake him. "We need to check his alibi."

Tanner placed the call. The Walmart manager confirmed that Martinez had worked the night shift. There were twelve guys who could attest to the fact he was there all night and never left the building.

"I'm going to pull the surveillance tapes, just to be sure," Tanner said.

Angela agreed that it couldn't hurt. Employees could be pretty loyal sometimes, and the tapes would show if Martinez had slipped out at any time during his shift.

"If it's not him, who else is on our list?" Tanner asked. "The husband?"

Ron Henderson hadn't been ruled out. They still needed to verify his whereabouts earlier in the evening, which meant a stop at Garcia's. There was also the alleged girlfriend to interview, plus they needed to know where Shelia Henderson had gone on the night she was murdered.

"Do you feel like a burger?" Angela asked. "Henderson said he was at Garcia's with colleagues until just before closing time. I hear they make a mean slider."

Chapter 7

Garcia's was a located in a strip mall off of Quebec St. and 58th, and the parking lot was packed. Most of the vehicles were pickups or beat up vans, with one or two lowriders tucked in. Happy Hour appeared to be in full swing. The music was so loud that the walls of the building appeared to pulse and Angela could feel the bass vibrate through the asphalt in the parking lot.

She scanned the console of the patrol car. "Do you have any earplugs in here?"

"Man up," Tanner said.

The customers in the parking lot eyed the two of them warily as they walked from the parking lot to the front door. Tanner reached for the handle.

"Allow me," he said.

"This isn't a date."

"I know. You're too old for me anyway, but what's wrong with showing some manners?"

Angela let him open the door for her and stepped inside. Most of the patrons looked like they belonged to a blue-collared, drinking crowd. Chairs were haphazardly pulled up to tables covered with pitchers, glasses and appetizer plates. Working their way over to a long wooden bar, Tanner commandeered two empty barstools and ordered a beer. She was surprised when the bartender didn't card the deputy, but asked to see her ID.

"Really?" She showed him her license, and then ordered a Diet Coke and a burger. "Heavy on the blue cheese, and with bacon."

"You got it." The bartender pointed to Tanner. "How about you?"

Tanner ordered a flauta and a water back.

"Busy in here today," Angela said when the bartender returned with her Coke.

"Always," he said, setting down her drink and Tanner's beer. "The food and water will be up in a few minutes."

"No rush," she said, "but we need to ask you a question."

The bartender made a face. A waitress down at the other end was signaling to him and at least three customers were holding out empty beer glasses. "It's going to have to wait."

Angela nodded and turned to Tanner. He was seated, but bopping his feet along to the beat.

"They're not bad," he said, gesturing to the band.

While they waited for the food to arrive, Angela scanned the bar crowd. The crowd was mostly white and Hispanic. The type of place an engineer and his crew might come. The type of place a person could let down after a hard day on the job. Maybe next time she'd try coming by on her day off.

Once the food arrived, Angela focused all her attention on the burger at hand. She hadn't realized how hungry she was, and couldn't remember the last time she had eaten. As she mopped up the ketchup with her last fry, the bartender materialized.

"I've got a few minutes," he said. "You want to step outside where it's easier to hear and I can have a smoke?"

Angela signaled to Tanner.

The sun was setting on the foothills when they reached the parking lot, painting the sky a deep red, and the temperature had dropped to a comfortable level. The bartender lit a cigarette.

"So what is it you want to know?"

Angela produced a picture of Ron Henderson. "Do you remember seeing this guy in here with a group of colleagues two nights ago?"

"I remember the dude, but I don't know if I'd call the woman he was with a colleague."

"A woman?" That supported Patty's allegations that he was seeing someone. "Can you describe her?"

"Let me clarify. The dude came in with a group, but the rest of them split pretty fast. He and the woman stayed until nearly one-thirty. I remember the time because it was last call. The dude wanted to go, but the chick wanted another drink. I didn't get out of here until two or so, and then the cops had me back here early that morning."

"What for?" Tanner asked.

Angela tamped down her annoyance at his veering off track. "What did the woman look like?"

"The shootings," the bartender said, answering Tanner's question. "Two guys were gunned down in our parking lot early the next morning."

Angela remembered the coroner saying something about a homicide. That had to be the case Detective Sykes was assigned. But two homicides on the same morning in Commerce City. What were the odds? Angela wondered if they were somehow connected.

"What did the cops want from you?" Tanner asked.

The bartender took another drag off his cigarette. "They showed me a couple of pictures of the guys and asked for the bar's surveillance tapes. They think one of the dudes left his car here the night before."

"Did you recognize either of the men?" Angela asked.

"Nah. The place was crowded that night and I had some company at the bar that was holding my attention, if you get my drift."

"Then how do you remember Henderson and the woman he was with?" Angela asked.

"Hey, she was all over the dude. I was about to suggest they get a room, when he went out to smoke a cigarette. He came back all flipped out. He sent the chick he was with out the back and he left through the front. I thought it was weird."

"Can you describe the woman he was with?"

"Average. She wasn't bad looking, but she wasn't great either."

"Hair color or eye color?" Tanner asked.

The bartender took a last drag on his cigarette and ground the butt into the asphalt. "She was a brunette. I prefer blondes."

That meant, whoever the woman Ron Henderson was with wasn't Sheila, thought Angela. "Can you remember anything else about her?"

"Sorry," the bartender said. "You want to know what someone's drinking, I can tell you that."

"What was she drinking?" Angela asked.

"He ordered beer. She was banging down gin and colas, no ice."

Angela couldn't help but make a face. It matched Tanner's.

"Dude, you'd be surprised at the things people order," the bartender said.

"Thanks," Tanner said, then sarcastically added, "Dude."

The bartender didn't notice, but it made Angela smile.

Chapter 8

It was dark by the time Angela and the deputy got back to her truck, but they had come up with a game plan. Tanner was going to check the surveillance tapes at the Walmart in the morning, while she went to see the alleged girlfriend, Ellie Parker.

The next morning, before heading out to the Parker residence, Angela called Patty Litchfield. If the she and Sheila were really best friends, it was possible the woman might know where the victim had gone on the night before she was murdered. Patty picked up on the first ring. Angela quickly identified herself.

The answer to her question was no.

Ellie Parker and her husband lived in the Reunion neighborhood of Commerce City—a little bit farther north and farther east than the area where the Henderson's lived. The houses looked the same, just larger and newer, with bigger yards. Angela had called ahead. Ellie was expecting her.

The woman who answered the door was tall and handsome, with dark hair pulled back into a low bun and dark eyes circled with eyeliner.

"Thanks for making time to see me this morning," Angela said.

"It's was a good excuse for me to stay home," Ellie said, leading her into a formal area with stiff-backed chairs and wall-to-wall bookcases on three side. Before they could sit, the phone rang.

"Wait here," Ellie gestured toward a straight-backed chair. "I'll be right back."

Instead of sitting, Angela walked over to the bookcases. Most of the shelves were filled with books—leather bound editions of the Law Review, some romance novels, a few mysteries and travel books—while other shelves held framed photographs and artifacts. The most interesting things were a grouping of Indian artifacts beside two framed photographs—one of a handsome Native American and one of a young boy.

"That's our son."

Angela hadn't seen any mention of children in her profile. "How old is he now?"

"He would be eight. Evan died shortly after that picture was taken."

"I'm sorry." The words seemed small by comparison to the grief Angela witnessed etched on Ellie's face.

"He developed leukemia. I've never been able to have any more children, though we've tried."

Hoping to put the interview back on solid footing, Angela pointed to the other photo. "Who is this?"

Ellie set down the picture of her son, and then brightened slightly when she touched the picture of the older man. "We think that is a picture of my husband's great-great-great-grandfather, Quanah Parker."

That piqued Angela's interest. "Your husband is Native American."

"He is," Ellie said, "though you would never know it." She walked over to where Angela stood and pointed to a large carved box sitting on the floor beside a small drum. "This is something passed down to him from his father. It's an old peyote box that belonged to his great-great-great-grandfather, Quanah Parker. Are you familiar with him?"

"He was a Comanche chief," Angela said.

"The last free Comanche chief. He was a famous warrior who led his people in battle against the white man, and then led them to surrender at Fort Sill."

If Angela remembered her history, he also negotiated land

settlements for his people that later generated large income through grazing leases. "Wasn't his mother a white woman?"

Ellie nodded. "Cynthia Ann Parker. She was captured during a Comanche raid when she was nine years-old. She grew up among the Indians and fell in love with Chief Peta Noconi. They had three children. When Quanah was still a young boy, his mother was retaken by Texas Rangers. History says she begged to be returned to the Comanche, and even tried escaping, but she was forced to live with her white relatives and eventually died of a broken heart. Quanah later took her surname in her honor."

"This is a museum piece."

"It most certainly is. My husband had this appraised and it's worth thousands. Each box was very individualized."

Ellie opened the box. Inside were a feather fan, a gourd rattle and a wooden stick with carvings that matched the rattle. The items were decorated with intricate beading. Four bald eagle tail feathers, two broken, hung from beading on the wooden rattle, while the fan was made of ten perfect bald eagle wing feathers bound together by hemp rope. Smudged with the resin and ash of century old fire, Angela could tell they were old.

In addition to the larger items, there were smaller, personal artifacts as well—a rosary, several arrowheads, several Indian head pennies, a small pearl stickpin and a photograph of a young white woman in Indian dress.

Ellie picked up the fan and handed it to Angela. "It's beautiful, isn't it?"

Angela admired the feathers and the beading. She'd seen similar artifacts come into the Repository, but nothing as spectacular as this.

"According to what I know," Ellie said, "Quanah Parker brought the peyote ceremony to the *Numinu*, the people. He and the men would gather in a tent, where there was an altar for the peyote button. Each man would bring his own peyote set, along with a drum. They would gather in a semi-circle around Father Peyote, and then they would drum and rattle and pray. And drink peyote tea and smoke hand-rolled cigarettes, of course. The fans were used to waft their prayers to the heavens. In the morning, the women would feed the men a feast and then they would all go home until the next time."

Angela handed Ellie back the fan and watched her gently place it back in the box. "If your husband's interested, we could catalog the contents and date the feathers to verify its authenticity."

Ellie smiled. "As romantic a notion as it is, he the son of an Indian chief and me his princess, he doesn't much care. He finds his heritage interesting and all, but he's an attorney and way too busy to give it much thought." Ellie again gestured at the grouping of chairs. "Now, what is it you wanted to see me about?"

Angela perched on the edge of her seat and decided to get right to the point. "I'm investigating the death of Sheila Henderson. It's been suggested by someone close to the investigation that you're close to the deceased's husband, Ron."

"We work together, if that's what you mean."

Angela tried to think of a delicate way to broach the subject of sleeping with another woman's husband. "Closer. We've been told that you and Mr. Henderson are intimately involved."

Ellie reared back in her chair. "Are you accusing me of having an affair with Ron?"

Angela pursed her lips and nodded.

"That's absurd. Who told you that?" Ellie's eyes flashed anger. "Ron would never do that."

"No," Angela answered.

"Someone else in my office?"

Angela leaned forward. "Why would you ask that?"

Ellie stood and paced the length of the room. "I'm a woman in a man's job. There are a number of my co-workers who still believe the only way a woman could climb the ladder as fast as I have is if I'm sleeping with the boss. Well, it's not true."

"So you're denying you and Ron have a special friendship."

"Not at all. He's been a great mentor and friend. We spend a lot of time together, just not in the way you're suggesting." She tucked back a stray lock of hair. "I am happily married, I love my work and I'm a dedicated engineer. I want to know who slandered my name."

Angela chose a different tack. "Were you with Ron at Garcia's bar two nights ago?"

Ellie frowned. "Along with three of our co-workers. We were celebrating the completion of one of the bridges we were building."

"Who else was there?"

Ellie rattled off five names.

"How long did you stay?"

"I don't know. I left early, before dinner. Ron and a couple of the guys were still there. You can ask them if you don't believe me."

"And you came straight home?"

"Yes. It was getting late, and I knew Sam would be wondering where I was."

* * *

After wrapping up with Ellie, Angela was ten minutes late meeting Deputy Tanner. She found him hunched over his computer watching a video replay.

"Anything," she asked.

"Oh, yeah," he said, hitting the rewind button. "Check this out."

He hit play again and the image of the Walmart parking lot appeared. The picture was grainy, but it showed a clear shot of a gray 4-Runner pulling into a parking space and Sheila Henderson climbing out and then disappearing into the store.

"It doesn't prove that she saw Ken Martinez," Angela said.

"Keep watching." Tanner hit fast forward, and then hit play again. This time there was a picture of Sheila exiting the store with Martinez behind her. They appeared to exchange words, before he went back inside and Sheila climbed into her car and drove away.

Martinez had lied to them about seeing Shelia the night she died. Why? "What time was that?"

"By the log, about one a.m."

Within the time frame of the head injury. "It looks like we'll need to talk with Mr. Martinez again."

"I agree," Tanner said, reaching for a stack of papers on his desk. "But that's not all I discovered. I found out something else interesting while I was poking around this morning. Remember how Martinez said that the vic was always suing people. I discovered that she has more than one lawsuit filed against the city." He held out the papers. "Take a look."

Angela took the pages and pulled up an empty chair. She didn't have to read far to realize they had just opened up their suspect pool.

A year ago, Sheila had filed a lawsuit against Commerce City and the U.S. Army. According to the document in Angela's hands, the woman claimed to hold the original deed to one-hundred sixty acres of Rocky Mountain Arsenal land; acreage later annexed by Commerce City. Sheila asserted that documentation she held proved that her family was never compensated for the land taken by the U.S. Army in 1942. She claimed that, as the Henderson's sole heir, she was therefore entitled to ownership and use of the land and/or payment and interest for the acreage in question. She was seeking in excess of one million dollars.

Angela flipped the page and found something of interest. In addition to Commerce City, one individual had recently been added to the suit; someone against whom Sheila was seeking personal damages—Carl Leeds, the mayor of Commerce City.

Angela looked up. "Isn't Carl Leeds up for reelection?"

"Next year," Tanner said. "I didn't think you could sue the government."

"There are liability limits and she'd need a damn good attorney." Angela turned to the back page and whistled.

"I think we need to talk to the esquire," Angela said.

"Who?"

"Sheila's attorney. Samuel Parker is listed as the attorney-of-record."

"The mistress's husband?" Tanner said.

Angela set the papers down on the corner of his desk. "Ellie claims that's a lie. She admitted to being at Garcia's that night, but says she left before all her co-workers did. We'll need to verify."

"I can do that, either before or after I go by Walmart and pay Ken Martinez a visit," Tanner said.

Angela stood and pushed back the chair. "I have to check in at the Repository and file some paperwork." She knew Wayne was probably already having a fit that she hadn't reported to work. The report to DOI was due before noon. "Let me know what Martinez says. Meanwhile, I'll schedule meetings with the mayor and Parker. I'll let you know the times."

Chapter 9

It was close to eleven-thirty by the time Angela reached the warehouse, and most of the staff was clocked out for lunch. It took her fifteen minutes to file the paperwork with the DOI, and nearly double the time on the phone to arrange the meetings with Parker and Leeds. Parker could meet with them at three p.m. Leeds was tied up until 5:00 p.m.

Angela texted Tanner the times, checked in with Wayne, and then headed downstairs to see what new cases had come in during the past few days. She had just reached the warehouse floor, when Detective Sykes walked through the door.

"Just the person I wanted to see," Sykes said.

Angela's curiosity piqued. The coroner's ruling of blunt force trauma made Shelia's death a homicide. Had Adams County reassigned the detective? "Are you back on the case?"

"No, still working the shooting. That's why I'm here."

Angela hadn't noticed the large brown bag he gripped in his hand until he held it out. "What's this?"

"We were searching the vic's car and found these." He thrust the bag into her hands. She took it and gingerly opened the sack. Inside was a jumbled mass of what looked like eagle feathers.

Moving to a steel table, she dumped out the contents and sorted them into order. All in all, she counted twelve tail feathers, twenty primary wing feathers and twenty-seven secondary wing feathers.

Her stomach grew queasy. "Where did you find these?"

"On the back seat of the vic's car. Why?"

"An eagle has thirty feathers. You're one shy. Except, yesterday, Wayne and I found a feather out by the eyrie. I think it matches these."

"An eyrie?"

"An eagles' nest. Hold on a minute. I want to retrieve the other feather."

She struggled to keep her emotions in check—a mixture of sadness that made her want to close in and anger which made her want to lash out. After what she'd just seen, there was no denying that something bad had happened to one of their pair of nesting eagles.

Grabbing the feather off of her desk, she pounded back down the stairs and slipped it into the mix. It was a perfect match to the same placement feather on the intact side. There was no doubt it belonged to the same eagle.

"You're sure it came from the same bird?" Sykes scratched his head. "What the heck were these guys doing with a bag of eagle feathers? They planning on making a headdress or something?"

"It's possible. Or maybe they planned to sell them. Eagle feathers are worth a lot on the black market. If they were planning on selling these, they could be charged under the Lacey Act. It protects bald eagles and can carry a felony charge and fines up to $250K."

Sykes whistled.

"You know, I'm beginning to believe that the shootings and Shelia Henderson's murder are connected," she said, even more after explaining the value of the bird for the second time in two days.

"What makes you say that?"

"The single feather was found in an area where Sheila had visited. She had to have gotten it from them."

"That's a stretch. She could have just found it, or maybe she didn't even know it was there."

"Or maybe she took it and got caught."

"Then why did my guys track her down and kill her and leave

the feather behind on the ground?" Sykes shook his head. "Your victim died from a blow to the noggin. Both of my guys had weapons on them, and so did the guy who shot 'em. If your vic had caught those bozos out here with the bird, why wouldn't they have just shot her?"

"Maybe they didn't want to risk a report of shots fired on the Refuge. Or maybe the blow to the head incapacitated her and they didn't need to shoot her." Angela was grasping at straws, but her gut was telling her somehow the two cases were linked. "If Sheila witnessed the men killing the bird, they easily might have murdered her to keep her quiet. Did either of the men have a record?"

"I see where you're going with this," Sykes said. "Yes, both men have long rap sheets. A felony charge would tag them both as habitual offenders. They could have been looking at life."

"There's your motive."

"Except, they already are. I've got 'em on illegal drug possession, illegal possession of firearms and unlawful weapons discharge. That's enough to put those boys away for a long time." Sykes picked up a feather. "You can't even tie your dead woman to the bird."

"Only by proximity."

Sykes put the feather down. "Not good enough. Now, you show me a rock solid connection between my two guys and the dead woman and I'll reconsider. Right now, even if the feather was found in her possession, any lousy attorney could say that she found it on the ground. Especially near a bird's nest. For that matter, without the carcass, who's to say that your gal and my guys didn't just find all these feathers?"

"You don't really believe that, do you?"

"No. But, until you find me a dead bird that I can connect to my vics, I'm going to leave you holding the bag." Sykes chuckled at his own joke, and then pointed to feathers.

"Seriously, what happens to these now?"

"I keep them here," Angela said, pulling the feather she'd added and setting it off to the side. "I'll tag the ones you brought in and hold them as evidence. You did the right thing, Sykes. Normally I'd be pressing charges against the person who'd been found in possession of these feathers. I take it he's dead?"

"The guy driving the car is dead. The passenger suffered a gunshot wound. He's in the hospital. I can't say for sure which one of them the bag belonged to. Maybe if we're lucky, our vic will be able to ID the man who shot him. Heck, for all I know, the shooter might be the one the feathers belong to."

"Do you have any witnesses?"

"A few folks who say the shooter took off on foot, but not one of them who could give me an accurate description. Most agree he was slight of build. We canvased the area, checked all the surveillance tapes and turned up nothing."

Angela was still thinking about how the two cases bisected. Maybe the connection between the two cases wasn't the Refuge or the bird. Maybe it was Garcia's.

"The bartender told me you confiscated the surveillance video," she said.

"Yeah, so what?"

"I'd like to look at them."

"What for?"

She gave him the straight answer. "Sheila Henderson's husband, Ron, was the last one to see her alive. We have witnesses that put him inside Garcia's the night before his wife's body was discovered. According to the bartender, he was there with a woman and they were very friendly. Then just before last call, Henderson went outside for a smoke. He must have seen something in the parking lot that spooked him. The bartender said he was really jumpy when he came back in, and that a few minutes later he sent his mystery woman out through the back while he left through the front."

"You're hoping to ID this nameless female."

"If I can. At the very least, it would be nice to figure out what scared Ron so badly that he cut short his date." While she was at it, she intended to check out the timeline on Sykes' victims, too. "Are the tapes any good?"

"Crystal clear. One of my vics parked his car at the backend of the lot and got into the other vic's car about nine p.m. They drove off and didn't come back until just after 7:00 a.m., just in time to get shot."

The timing fit her case, too—provided Ron Henderson was telling the truth about seeing Sheila at home that morning. If she had gone straight out to the Refuge at 6:00 a.m., she could easily have crossed paths with the two men.

Angela glanced at the clock. It was getting late, and she had an appointment to go to.

"Thanks for bringing these by, Sykes." Angela picked up a camera and snapped several photos of the feathers. "How does if fit if I come by the office tomorrow to look at the tapes?"

"Anytime works. I'll make sure they're on the computer, just in case I'm out. Tanner can access them for you. I can't let you have the originals. Chain of custody, and all that."

"Not a problem." All she wanted to do was fill in the time gaps, and she could do that just as easily at the Adam's Co. Sheriff's Department as here.

Sykes rapped his knuckle against the steel table, signaling he was ready to leave. "Anything else you need from me?"

"Yes," Angela said, reaching for a pen. "I'd like the names of the victims in your case."

Sykes frowned. "What for?"

"So I can file charges against the one that's still alive."

"His name is Patrick Begay, age twenty-seven. His buddy's name was Donny Smith."

"Any chance I can talk with Begay?"

"Stand in line. Right now he has a breathing tube shoved down his throat and he hasn't regained consciousness."

* * *

The law offices of Parker & Hall were located on the third floor of a ten-story high-rise off of Quebec, just south of I-70, across from a new upscale development in the old Stapleton area. The attorney's names were stenciled in white on the glass door and a perky receptionist manned the front desk.

"May I help you?"

Angela handed her a card. "Special Agent Angela Dimato of US Fish and Wildlife and Deputy Tanner from Adams County Sheriff's department. We're here to see Sam Parker."

"Have a seat," the receptionist said. "I'll let him know you're here."

Angela sat opposite Tanner in a large, plush oversized chair that made her feel trapped. The color scheme was pale gray, with giant John Fielder photographs of Colorado adorning the walls. On the back wall were two large, gilt-framed paintings of two men. She assumed the man on the left was Parker and the other one Hall.

Parker stared back from the canvas from wide-set eyes, over high cheek bones and a long nose. She was struck by the facial resemblance to the photograph on his bookcase of Quanah Parker, even though in the painting his dark hair was cut short.

"A little ostentatious for my tastes," said a man behind her.

She turned to find Sam Parker standing behind her. "It's a good likeness."

"My partner's idea."

Parker stood over six feet. An imposing man, he was dressed in khaki's, a blue oxford shirt opened at the collar and a charcoal sports coat.

"Follow me to my office," he said, and then once they were settled, "Now, what can I do for you?"

"We understand that you represent Sheila Henderson in several lawsuits. One against the city, the school district and Ken Martinez, and one against the City and U.S. Army."

"Both are a matter of public record."

"She's dead," Tanner said.

Parker's gaze sharpened, more hawkish. "Also a matter of public knowledge."

Angela shifted in her seat. "Mr. Parker, we're trying to find out who might have wanted your client dead. Can you tell us a little more about the lawsuit?"

Parker picked up a pencil from his desk and twirled it in his fingers. "I'm sure you've read the filings."

Angela could tell he was deliberately making this difficult. What her father would have called *playing it close to the vest*. "Let's start with the case Sheila brought against the U.S. Army and Commerce City."

Parker balanced the pencil on the end of his index finger. "Sheila holds ownership of one-hundred sixty acres of Rocky Mountain Arsenal land. Her family was never properly compensated and the documents of ownership never turned over. The case is solid."

"How did the government react to the suit?" Angela asked.

"They think it's frivolous." Parker flipped the pencil into the air, caught it firmly in his fist, and then let it roll off the palm of his hand onto the desk. "Frankly, Agent Dimato, I don't want to tip my hand to you. Based on your connection to the Refuge and Deputy Tanner's connection to Adams County, I think telling the two of you anything could compromise my ability to use certain information in court."

Tanner leaned forward, his posture threatening. "This is a

murder investigation, Mr. Parker. We expect some answers. Don't make me hit you with obstruction charges."

Angela cringed. Parker laughed.

"You've been watching too much crime TV, officer."

"Deputy," Tanner corrected.

Parker lounged back in his chair. "You must understand, Deputy. My obligation is to my client."

"But as we've pointed out," Tanner said, "she's dead."

Parker scooted his chair in and gripped the edge of his desk. "But her heirs aren't. I've already spoken with her husband about going forward with the case. He's agreed we should pursue it. Unfortunately, I am compelled to protect my client's interest in this matter and I am under no obligation to share any information with you."

"Maybe we need to speak with your client," Tanner said.

"If Ron will talk with you and wishes to share details of the case, that's his prerogative. Though, be assured, I will advise him against it."

Tanner started to speak, but Angela stopped him. "Fair enough, Mr. Parker. What about Sheila's other case, the one against the school district and city regarding the soccer fields?"

"It's in mediation."

That meant they were nearing a settlement of some sort. "Does she have any other cases pending?"

"That information is confidential."

"I'll take that as a yes," Angela said, annoyed at his stonewalling.

"This has been a waste of time," Tanner said, pushing to his feet. "You haven't told us anything."

"That's a matter of perspective," Parker said. "I haven't wasted my time, because there is something we need to clarify."

Angela was gripped by a sense of unease. "What's that?"

"You came by my house this morning to speak with my wife."

It didn't surprise her that Ellie had told him about the visit. "I did."

"From here on out, if you have any questions for my wife, you are to contact me. While she is happy to cooperate, she felt the tone of your conversation was accusatory. Any further conversations will be conducted with either me or a member of my firm present." Parker stood and handed her a card. "Is that understood?"

Knowing he was only protecting his wife and client, Angela struggled to mask her dislike for the man. His tactics epitomized what she liked least about lawyers—most of them had a kill instinct that rivaled a badger's. Reaching out she took the card and tucked it into her pocket. "I'm sure that we'll have more questions, Mr. Parker. Count on my being in touch."

Chapter 10

The meeting at the mayor's offices was bound to go better. Angela and Tanner arrived early, and the reception area was utilitarian and familiar enough to place her on solid ground. The walls were painted institutional beige. Here, ten-by-twelve photographs of the council members graced one wall, flanked on either side by the U.S. and state of Colorado flags, and cushioned metal chairs sat in two-columns on the white-tiled floors.

Angela strode down the wide aisle that opened to the curved receptionist's desk, and asked the skinny woman manning the desk if Mayor Leed was in.

The woman looked up and smiled. "He's here and waiting."

She was already dialing the phone, and the mayor appeared before they had time to sit down.

"Welcome." Mayor Leed dressed the part. He wore a blue suit with a navy and red barber-pole stripped tie, and glad-handed both of them in the typical fashion of a politician up for reelection. "I'm pleased to know that you're being thorough about looking into Sheila Henderson's death. That poor woman. She had some issues, and sure made a lot of folks angry."

"That's the main reason we're here," Angela said.

Tanner nodded. "We want to know if someone had it in for her."

Angela maintained a straight face and studied the mayor's reaction. While there was no question the deputy needed to learn some tact, she was beginning to appreciate the effect his blunt statements had on people.

Mayor Leed seemed visibly shaken. Glancing around the reception area, he gestured for them to follow him down the hallway into a barebones conference room and shut the door.

"She upset a lot of people," he said once they were seated. "But I honestly don't know anyone, at least not anyone from my office that wanted her harmed."

"Not even you," Tanner asked. "She pointed the finger at you in at least one lawsuit."

The deputy was on a roll. "Mayor, where do the lawsuits stand?" Angela asked.

Leed wiggled in his a chair at the head of the table. His ample body filled the seat and sweat beaded on his tanned forehead. "I take it you know about both of them?"

Angela nodded.

Leed planted his elbows on the table. Folding his hands together, he leaned in. "At the end of the school year, pending an outcome of an investigation I ordered into the condition of the fields, the city council and school district voted to suspend the Adams County school district's soccer program. As the governing body in Adams County, the city council takes its role as stewards of our community very seriously."

Angela listened to him drone on with the political rhetoric for a moment, and then cut him off with another question. "How did the community react?"

"They didn't like the decision. But as city council, sometimes we have to make wise, prudent calls in the face of opposition, for the betterment of our citizens."

In other words, the city council couldn't afford to take the risk of another student being injured and another lawsuit being filed.

"Who was the maddest?" Tanner asked.

Mayor Leed didn't miss a beat. "Ken Martinez. He claimed that we had caved-in on the soccer issue because of the other litigation. He's threatened to file recall petitions for all the council members, myself included."

"Isn't this an election year?" Angela asked.

"Yes, it is. And I won't deny that Sheila Henderson has made it a nightmare. The condition of our soccer fields is a minor problem when compared with the real issues facing our community. We need to be focused on job growth, commercial growth and diminishing train noise. That's a place where we've made strides. Yet, the soccer issue has taken the forefront. It's all anybody wants to talk about."

"And that case goes away with Sheila Henderson dead," Tanner said.

"If only it were that easy." Leed reached up and loosened his tie. "But we think we may have a solution. We're planning on announcing it at tonight's council meeting."

"Can we get a preview?" Angela asked.

Leed hesitated. Tanner opened his mouth to speak, but Angela silenced him with a hand gesture. The silence stretched uncomfortably in the small conference room, until finally Leed broke.

"Dick's Sporting Good Park has agreed to open up its soccer fields on a limited basis for practices and games. We believe if we combine the programs in the district, require tryouts and cut members to form the teams that we'll be able to field at least two high school teams eligible to participate in state competitions."

"That's a creative solution," Angela said. "Did you come up with that?"

Leed preened. "I facilitated the discussions and approached Dick's with the idea."

"In other words, no," Tanner said.

The mayor pulled a handkerchief from his pocket and mopped his brow. "It was Martinez's idea."

It seemed that rather than expend his energy on seeking revenge, Ken Martinez had sought and found a solution to the problem for Ken Jr. It spoke well of his character, thought Angela, but it didn't explain why he lied about seeing Sheila

Henderson the night before she was found dead.

"What about the second lawsuit, Mayor Leed? The one that names you as a defendant," Angela asked.

Again the silence stretched. The room was getting stuffy, and Angela wished Leed would crack the door or offer them some water. On the other hand, she didn't want the spirit of cooperation, driven by Leed's apparent discomfort, broken. She pressed.

"Do you know what's going to happen with the second lawsuit?"

"I'm hoping the matter will be dropped."

Parker had just told them that the lawsuit would be going forward on Leroy Henderson's behalf. Mayor Leed must not have gotten the word.

"Better luck next time," Tanner said.

Leed wiped the politician's smile off his face and looked from Tanner to Angela. She smiled sympathetically.

"We just came from Sam Parker's office, Mayor," she said. "Nothing's changed."

The Mayor looked stunned. Like a puffer fish out of water, his mouth gapped open and working, then his face deepened to a dark red color and he slammed a fist down on the table. "*Damn*! That bitch has caused me more trouble. Even from the grave she makes my life difficult."

A lament that killing her hadn't worked, or simply an acknowledgement that the problems he hoped would resolve because of her death had just resurface?

Looking up, the mayor seemed to realize the effect of his outburst. "I apologize for my emotion. It's just that there are much more important things to be addressed in Commerce City and much better ways to spend taxpayers' money than defending ourselves against a frivolous lawsuit brought by a woman who seemed to thrive on discord and attention."

"Things like 'train noise?'" Tanner asked.

"You mock, but it was listed as the number three concern of our citizens last year. We believe we've solved that problem by creating quiet zones." Leed was back in full politician mode. "On the 96th street crossing we installed an Automated Horn System, the first of its kind in Colorado. It's a device, mounted on a pole at the crossings rather than on the locomotive, that cuts the noise pollution in our neighborhoods for more than 1.5 miles along the tracks at a minimal cost of eight million dollars."

"You said the other concerns were jobs and commercial developments," Angela said.

"That's right. Gang activity is something that's on our radar, too. Like the shootings the other night. Those young men were both thought to be gang members, and the shootings appear to be tied to some sort of outside criminal activity."

One being possible violations of the Bald Eagle Protection Act of 1940 and the Lacey Act.

"Are there any other council members who feel as passionately as you about Sheila Henderson's lawsuits, Mayor?" Angela asked.

"All of us feel strongly about this," Leed said. "If her suit goes forward and we're forced to pay a settlement for something that happened back in the 1940s, it would significantly impact our budget. It would make it nearly impossible for us to implement any of things we have slated for the upcoming years." He threw his hands up. "Giving her the land is not an option. No, it's our position that if anyone has to pay recompense it's the U.S. Army. They were the ones who didn't handle this properly by not making payment and not filing the right documents in the first place."

The position made sense to Angela, but then she didn't know the specifics of the case. The outcome seemed destined to end with the court.

"You want to know what I think," Tanner said. "Either way it's the taxpayers who are getting screwed."

"A very astute observation, Deputy." Leed flashed his politician's smile, apparently regaining his equilibrium. "Now, have I answered all of your questions?"

"Just one more thing," Angela said. "Where were you two nights ago between the hours of midnight and eight a.m.?"

Leed knitted his eyebrows in surprise. "Home."

"Can anyone verify that?" Tanner asked.

The mayor looked uncomfortable and tugged as his tie again. "No. You see, I live alone. My wife and I are separated. One of the hazards of being a public servant, I'm afraid. She didn't like the hours."

Chapter 11

Angela reported to work the next morning and brought Wayne up to speed on the investigation. After filing paperwork for the DOI, she worked on the backlog of receipts and requests that had come into the Repository in the last three days. On average the Repository received six shipments a day of either whole birds or parts and fielded eleven requests for birds or parts from across the United States. There was nearly double the demand than there was supply, and each receipt of an eagle or part required an investigation to ensure no illegal activity had taken place in the act of acquiring.

At noon she ducked out and grabbed lunch, then headed for the Adams County Sheriff's Office. Pushing through the front door, she found the common area of the squad room practically empty. Deputy Tanner sat alone at his station, typing up reports.

Sitting in an adjoining desk chair, she wheeled herself over beside his desk. "Did you have a chance to follow up with Ken Martinez?"

"Yeah." Tanner kept typing.

"What did he have to say?"

"He claimed that he bumped into the vic in electronics. Henderson came in, and when she saw him she went on the defensive. They exchanged a few words, and then he told her that she didn't need to worry about it anymore. He explained that the city council had found a solution."

"So he was aware of the mayor's negotiations?"

"Apparently."

"Did he say why he didn't tell us he had run into Sheila?"

Tanner stopped tapping on the keys and looked up. "He said he thought it would make us more suspicious, given his previous threats."

"He was right."

"Yeah, but from what I can see, it looks like he's in the clear." Tanner went back to typing. "He never left the building or grounds. Not until the next morning."

Angela settled back in the chair. "One down."

Tanner tapped two more keys, then clicked the mouse and sat back in his chair. "Done."

"What about Mayor Leed?"

"I canvased his neighbors. One woman who lives across the street says she saw him come in around dusk and that his car was parked in his driveway all night."

"How can she be sure?" Angela asked. "She couldn't have had eyes on it the whole time."

"She has a dog that she regularly walks. The last time she went out was just before heading to bed at 2:00 a.m. According to her, Leed's car was still parked in the same spot."

"That doesn't mean he didn't go out," Angela said. But it did mean that he wasn't looking good for committing the crime. Without additional evidence or something that pointed directly to him, they were down to the husband and mystery woman, and Begay.

"Let's look at the surveillance tapes from Garcia's," Angela said. "Where's Detective Sykes?"

"The shooting victim came to this morning. Sykes headed to the hospital."

Angela felt a surge of excitement. "Is the guy talking?"

"Sykes didn't say, just that the victim had opened his eyes." Tanner leaned back over his computer. "As for the surveillance tapes, I should be able to pull them up on my computer provided Sykes logged them in correctly." He tapped a few keys. "Yeah, here they are."

Angela felt torn between looking at the tapes and heading

directly to the hospital to talk with Patrick Begay, but it made sense to check out the tapes first. She pulled her chair in close beside Tanner and leaned neck-and-neck toward the monitor. "Can you pick it up around eight-thirty p.m.?"

"Why so early?" Tanner asked queueing up the film.

"That's when Sykes said the two shooting victims met in the parking lot. I want to see if there's anything, or anyone, who appears suspicious on the tape."

Grainy black-and-white images scurried across the monitor. At around 9:00 p.m., Donny Smith pulled into the parking lot, parked and idled. Patrick Begay arrived shortly afterwards, parked, locked up his vehicle, and then climbed into Smith's car. The two drove out of the parking lot. Just like Sykes had told them.

"Now fast-forward to 1:00 a.m.," Angela said. "That's about the time Ron Henderson went out front."

As he closed in on the time, Tanner slowed the playback. Angela watched the images move on the screen. Still in faster motion than normal, the patrons in the parking lot looked like swift moving mannequins.

"Wait," she said, pointing at the screen. "There."

Tanner backed up the footage and hit play.

At 1:05 a.m., Ron Henderson exited the bar, pulled a cigarette out of a pack he pulled from his shirt pocket and fished a lighter from his pocket.

Angela scanned the cars in the parking lot. Near the back, in the dark shadows cast by the trees, she spotted Sheila's 4-Runner.

"There." Angela pointed. "Her car is in the right hand corner. Can you tell if she's inside the vehicle?"

Tanner zoomed in on the spot. Sheila was sitting in the driver's seat. Holding up a camera, she snapped a photo.

Ron seemed to notice her about the same time Angela had.

Dropping his cigarette, he ground it out on the sidewalk and went back inside. Shelia got out of her vehicle, crossed the parking lot and walked around the side of Garcia's to the back.

Had she figured out that Ron had seen her? She must have figured he would try and escape out the back.

"What's behind the bar?" Angela asked. "Do they have a camera on the backdoor?"

Tanner pulled up a list of the video files.

"Nothing here," he said.

Angela took the list out of his hands. "There has to be a camera that shows the back entrance?"

"I didn't find it listed."

Neither did Angela. She threw the list down on the desk. "*Damn.* Well, at least we know where Sheila went after Walmart." Angela pushed away from the desk. "Martinez told you she was in the electronics section, right? Did he tell you what she bought?"

"A camera."

"Tell me someone has the camera. Did they find it inside her car?"

Taylor rummaged on his desk and came up with two copies of the preliminary report from the CSI processing unit. "It came in just before you got her."

The two of them skimmed the report.

No camera. The only items cataloged in addition to the typical contents of a glove compartment were a box of tissues, a pair of binoculars, a spotting scope and an umbrella. The only prints they found belonged to either her or her son.

"Guess we need to talk to her husband again," Tanner said. "She probably took it home with her."

"Unless she dropped it, or gave it to someone else for safekeeping," Angela said. The idea niggled in the back of her mind. The two possibilities were her attorney, Sam Parker, or her BFF, Patty Litchfield. "We know she was taking pictures of Ron, and that she walked around back of Garcia's. What if she saw Ron's friend exiting and recognized her? Maybe the girlfriend hit her with something and took the camera."

"Makes sense to me," Tanner said. "For that matter, Sheila could have gone home and confronted Ron and they could have fought over the camera."

Angela pushed to her feet. "Let's not forget the other possibility. That she had it with her in the Refuge and took picture of something or someone, pictures that got her killed."

"If Ron's girlfriend took it, she might have ditched it in back of the bar. There's a dumpster back there."

"It's worth taking a look," Angela said. "I also think it's time we speak to Ron Henderson again."

The dumpster-diving came top of the list. If the trash hadn't already been picked up, time of the essence. The search proved futile. Tanner had climbed into the eight-foot roll-off and rummaged around, and come up empty handed. In his words, an 'epic fail.'"

Their next stop had been Henderson's. So far he hadn't lawyered up in relation to his wife's death, so they were free to try and talk with him. No one was at home.

Back in the patrol car, Tanner kicked on the air-conditioning. The temperature outside had climbed to over ninety and the wet rings in his armpits had expanded until they were visible. Angela wondered if she suffered the same fate, but opted not to look.

"We could head out to the Refuge and see if we can find the camera out there," Angela said.

"And scour all fifteen acres? Since it wasn't found with Sheila or at the First Creek site or where her car was located, it could be anywhere." Tanner narrowed his eyes at her. "What makes you so hot on proving there's a link between the two murders, anyway? The only thing you have linking the two cases is the random feather you found near the eyrie."

"A feather that matches the feathers found in the back of Smith's car. That means both victims were at the First Creek site."

"It could be just a coincidence," Tanner said.

"I don't believe in coincidences." Angela knew how clichéd that sounded. "We need to check the evidence log for Smith's car. Maybe they found a camera."

"Consider it done," Tanner said, shifting the patrol car into drive and pulling away from the curb. "I'll get on that first thing, when I'm back in the office. Meanwhile, let's go talk to Patrick Begay."

* * *

Denver Health Medical Center, located on Bannock Street in Denver, held a longtime reputation for being one of the best trauma hospitals in the country. Founded in 1860, one of its first patients had been a doctor, who had been badly injured in a duel. The violent nature of the injury and the doctor's subsequent care had cemented Denver Health's reputation as the "best place in Colorado to be treated for a gunshot wound."

Angela figured it also helped that for most of the next one hundred-fifty years all of the hard trauma cases had been delivered to their emergency bays. *Practice makes perfect.*

The jail lockdown unit was located on the bottom floors of the new Western Addition. Angela wasn't impressed. The state of the art facility had all the bells and whistles, but the unit was still in the basement. Artificial light gleamed off of white-tile floors and drab beige walls.

At the guard station at the end of a hallway leading to a set of closed double doors, Angela flashed her credentials.

"We're here to see Patrick Begay," she said to the officer on duty.

The officer took her badge and studied it, then handed her a clipboard. "You'll both need to sign-in here. Once I let you through, you'll need to check-in with the nurse. Only authorized personnel are allowed in and out, and only two visitors at a time per patient."

Angela scribbled her name and the time on sign-in sheet and handed the clipboard to Tanner. "Is Detective Sykes still here?"

"I don't know a Detective Sykes, ma'am. Again check with the nurse. She can tell you."

Tanner handed back the clipboard, then the officer made a phone call.

"You're good to go," he said. Gesturing for them to follow, he led them over to the double doors, swiped a card through the magnetic strip reader on the door, keyed in a four digit code and let them pass.

Once inside the unit, Angela assessed the layout. The detention area consisted of fourteen rooms positioned in a semi-circle around a central nurses' station. The two rooms closest to the entry door were double occupancy rooms and empty. The other twelve were private rooms, mostly empty. A large white board on the south wall listed bed assignments and patient names. Only six beds were in use. Begay was in room number ten.

The nurse was busy with another patient, so Angela took that as a sign and entered Begay's room. Tanner followed. They stepped up on either side of the bed.

Begay fit the definition of a trauma patient. After the bandage that swaddled his head, the bandages across his chest and abdomen and the PICC line in his chest, the first thing she noticed was that he was handcuffed to the bed. The second thing she noticed was how small he seemed.

"Patrick Begay," she said.

The man in the bed stirred and opened his eyes. "Who are you?"

Angela introduced herself and Deputy Tanner. "We have a few questions about the eagle feathers discovered in your car."

"I don't know nothing."

"Do you know who shot you?" Tanner asked.

"Like I told that other cop, I don't know nothing. And I'm not talking to nobody. I want you to get out." He rattled the handcuff chain against the rail of his bed. "Did you hear me?"

"Calm down, Begay," Angela said. "If you answer our questions, maybe we can help you."

"I don't need your help. I need you to get the hell out of here." Begay rattled his chains louder.

"Where did you get the eagle feathers?" Angela asked again.

"I have a right to have them. I am *Tsétsêhéstaestse*, Cheyenne."

"That doesn't give you the right to take feathers," Angela said.

Begay's face hardened. "Those feathers belong to the church."

"Yeah, what church is that?" Tanner asked.

"The Native American Church." Begay drilled Angela with a defiant stare. "Last I checked we still have a right to religious freedom in this country."

"You're right, but religious freedom doesn't trump federal law. Those feathers were newly harvested, taken without a permit. For a first offense, you're looking at a year in jail and a minimum ten-thousand dollar fine. If the judge throws the book at you, you could be facing a two hundred fifty-thousand dollar fine."

"Not to mention life in prison for the murder of Shelia Henderson," Tanner said.

Begay whipped his head around, and then winced. "What you

talkin' about? We didn't kill nobody. I'm the one who got shot."

"And we're still waiting for you to tell us who shot you," Tanner said.

"I don't know, okay? I didn't see. But I'm not going to lie here and let you pin a murder wrap on me. We didn't hurt nobody."

Angela pulled out a picture of Shelia Henderson. "Have you ever seen this woman?"

Begay squinted at the picture. "Is she dead? She looks dead."

"As a doornail," Tanner said.

Begay pushed the picture away, the handcuff chain clanging against the bed. "I ain't never seen her before. That's the truth." His skin grew paler with each sentence, and Angela wondered if he was lying or if that they might be taxing him too much. Suddenly a nurse appeared in the doorway.

"What are you doing in here?" she demanded, charging into the room. "Mr. Begay is not allowed visitors."

"A detective from our office was just here," Tanner said, "You were busy when we arrived."

"I don't care if I was invisible," the nurse said, herding them into the hall. "All visitors are required to check with the nurses' station before entering any patient's room. What part of before don't you understand?"

Angela felt her cheeks flush.

The nurse put her hands on her hips. "Now, who are you?"

Angela introduced herself and Deputy Tanner. "Begay is a suspect in a federal crime. We needed to ask him a few questions, and I was informed that he had regained consciousness."

"You and that other detective."

Angela figured she referred to Detective Sykes.

"Like I told him," the nurse continued, holding up three fingers. "Mr. Begay has sustained three gunshot wounds—one to the head, one to the chest and one to the abdomen. The shot to the chest collapsed one of his lungs and creased the left side of his liver causing massive internal bleeding. He might be awake, but he doesn't need you badgering him yet. I suggest you go back to your office and wait until you're officially notified that Mr. Begay is well enough to answer questions. Meanwhile, let me give you the name of his attorney."

Begay had lawyered-up? Angela glanced at Tanner.

"That sucks," he said.

The nurse walked over and rummaged around on her desk, then came up with a card and handed it to Angela. On one side, in embossed lettering was the name: Samuel Bernel Parker, Esq.

"That man gets around," Tanner said.

Chapter 12

By the time Angela and Tanner got back to the Adams County Sheriff's Office, Detective Sykes had clocked out for the day. That meant they would have to wait to ask him about whether or not a camera had been found in Smith's car.

Angela left a note on his desk, and then headed home. Bone-tired after the last four days, she ate, showered and tumbled into bed. She was at her desk the next morning before 7:00 a.m. She needed to file an update with the Department of Interior. To organize her thoughts, she ran through the case.

There were several possible suspects. None of them a threat to national security. Ken Martinez had all but been ruled out. Mayor Leed's alibi was shaky, but he didn't look good for the murder either. Ellie Parker's alibi had checked out. Not only had her co-workers backed up her story, but she was seen leaving on the surveillance tapes and was alibied by her husband.

That left Ron Henderson and the mysterious woman who accompanied him to Garcia's at the top of the list. Ron Henderson had gone home shortly after being spooked outside the bar. Jessie Martinez, the babysitter, could confirm that. But Angela had no way of knowing what happened out back of Garcia's between Sheila and the mysterious woman, or between Ron and Sheila later that night. As was often the case, it was looking more and more like the husband did it.

Then there were Smith and Begay, and their mysterious accomplice and possible shooter.

Interestingly, in both cases, Sam Parker's name came up. He represented Ron Henderson in the lawsuits against the city and he represented Begay.

Angela booted up her computer and Googled the attorney.

Samuel Bernal Parker was listed as a graduate of the University of Denver, Sturm College of Law. For several years after graduation he worked as a staff attorney at the American Civil Liberties Union of Colorado, before opening his own law practice five years ago. Since then he had litigated a preponderance of cases involving civil liberties, such as: gay equality, criminal justice, immigration rights, government transparency, and freedom of expression and religion.

From his own press, it sounded like everyone loved him.

Pulling up public records on his cases, one in particular drew her attention. Several years back, Parker had represented two Native American Church members who had been fired from their jobs for their use of peyote. They had filed claims for unemployment compensation and been turned down because they had been dismissed from their jobs for "misconduct." Despite the support of a number of religious organizations that reasoned that their right to free exercise of religion should allow their religious use of the drug, the court upheld the denial on the grounds that their job required them to remain drug-free. Ultimately the case had landed in the U.S. Supreme Court, which upheld the lower court's findings.

Parker had lost.

Her curiosity piqued, Angela conducted a keyword search for "The Native American Church."

Just as Ellie Parker had said, Sam Parker's reputed great-great-great-grandfather Quanah Parker had been central to the founding of the church. While traveling, he had taken the "medicine" for a difficult illness or injury, became a leading advocate of peyote, and was instrumental in turning back laws that would have forbidden its use.

According to the official website of the Native American Church, its philosophy represented a fusion of Christianity with traditional American Indian religions in varying degrees.

Peyote was regarded as a sacramental substance with divine powers—a "teacher." Vomiting was seen as a cleansing of the impurities present in the mind and body of the user. The psychoactive qualities were believed to enhance one's thinking and behavior. And, not only did peyote have medicinal effects, it deterred the desire for alcohol. Peyote was considered a cure for alcoholism.

The description of the peyote ceremony was also like Ellie had described it, with one exception—now women were welcomed at the ceremonies. At midevening, church members of all genders gathered around an altar inside a teepee. One man, called the road man, presided over the ceremony. He faced east. The cedar man threw chips on the fire to create a cleansing smoke, and then participants passed around peyote cactus and tea. Going around the circle, traditional songs were sung. At midnight, a water woman brought water and there was a break in the ceremony. Then participants reconvened, more songs were sung, prayers were offered, and sometimes healing ceremonies were conducted. At dawn, the road man sang the Dawn Song, the water woman brought more water, and the ceremony ended.

It sounded to Angela like a reason to get high. But, according to their literature, the church had an estimated two hundred fifty-thousand members. Not all of them could be stoners.

"Find out anything interesting?" a voice asked from the doorway. Angela looked up to find Wayne, leaning against the doorjamb.

She told him what she knew.

"Maybe you need to talk with Sam Parker again," Wayne said.

"And ask him what? He's not going to incriminate either of his clients, or compel either of them to talk."

"Does he represent the husband in the matter of his wife's death?"

"Not that I'm aware of." Which meant, technically she could still talk to him about the Sheila's death without going through his attorney. "What I really need is a warrant to search the Henderson house for the camera."

"Can Deputy Tanner arrange for one?"

"I'll ask."

"What about the murder weapon?"

"Undetermined. The coroner ruled out the steering wheel." She could check the alley in back of Garcia's again.

"Any other leads?"

"I suppose it could have something to do with the lawsuit over the land she claims is still hers."

"Sheila Henderson vs. the U.S. Army et al. Forget that," Wayne said. "Focus on the husband. Find that mystery woman of his and you'll have your answers."

So much easier said than done.

After checking the backlog of work at the National Eagle Repository, Angela opted to ignore Wayne's advice and pulled up what information she could on the Arsenal land Sheila Henderson claimed she still owned.

Homesteaded by Charles M. Eli out of Kansas City, Missouri records showed that he, his wife and three offspring had farmed a piece of property in Section 6 and 5, near the mouth of First Creek. Right near the area where Sheila's body had been found.

Angela accessed the historical data on the Arsenal and pulled up an old survey that showed the approximate location. From the markings on the map, it would include part of the eagles' roost and the eagles' nest.

According to an article in the *Rocky Mountain News*, Eli's great-great-great-grandson and Sheila's great-grandfather was still farming the land in 1942, when he and his family were forcibly removed by the U.S. Army. A more recent article in

The Denver Post digging into the dispute indicated that no official survey of the property boundaries had ever been done. It also noted that this was the same area where some of the sarin bomblets had been discovered.

Maybe the reason Sheila was so interested in the eagle's roost had nothing to do with the birds and everything to do with denoting the boundaries of her ancestral land. Maybe in the process of exploring the boundaries, she had stumbled upon something she shouldn't.

Making a copy of the survey map, Angela went to find Wayne. He was out, so she scribbled a note telling him what she'd discovered and left it for him on his desk. If Sheila had discovered something that had gotten her killed, Angela figured at least one person should know where she was headed. From the truck, she tried calling Tanner, but the call when straight to voice mail. *So much for backup.*

Angela parked her truck in the turnaround where they'd seen signs of a scuffle and re-canvased the area. This time she knew exactly what she was looking for—a weapon that might have been used to hit Sheila in the head; an eagle carcass, which would explain the eagle feathers found in Begay's possession; and a camera that may or may not contain incriminating photographs.

Taking a closer look around the area where the scuffle had taken place, Angela found one or two branches pitched aside that could have served as a club. None showed any evidence connecting it with a human head—no blood, no latent hairs. She then walked both sides of the stand of trees with the eagles' nest, and found nothing.

Taking a closer look at the map, she located the approximate southern boundary of the Eli acreage and walked it, cutting straight west from the nesting tree and crossing Chambers. The land here was covered in short grass—blue grama, buffalo grass and sagewort—and dotted with purple pasture thistle. She jumped First Creek, which here amounted to little more than a ditch with a trickle of water bordered on both sides with slightly greener vegetation. Two hundred feet more, she came to the edge of a small tributary and turned north.

She walked along the edge of the tributary and stopped underneath a small stand of Cottonwoods to scan the fields. The deer droppings on the trail were the only indication anything or anyone had been there.

Continuing north to the split of the creek, she stopped. The western boundary of the Eli homestead fell outside the vegetation growing along the creek. Large Cottonwoods, willows and a thicket of wild plums mixed with skunkbrush crowded the creek banks, and Angela skirted the tangle on the outside.

This had been a waste of time, she thought. Wayne was right. There was nothing here.

No sooner had her thoughts passed when she spotted a trampled area and broken branches leading toward the creek. Squatting, she studied the ground. Several partial boot prints were etched into the ground. She caught herself smiling. The disturbance was recent. This July, Colorado had seen its share of warm and dry weather; but on the weekend prior to Sheila's murder a front moving through had brought afternoon rains and windy conditions. The presence of boot prints now meant that whoever had been here had been here in the past five days.

It also meant that whoever had visited the creek had done so in violation of posted orders. It could easily have been kids in search of a secluded place to make out, but Sheila's gut told her it had something to do with why Sheila Henderson had ended up dead.

Angela snapped a few pictures, then stepped over the footprints and pushed her way through the crush of branches.

Once past the tangle of branches, the vegetation through the trees opened up and she slowed her pace, listening for sounds. All was quiet, except for a woodpecker somewhere in the trees above her.

Pushing through another tight section of thicket, she reached a clearing on the edge of the creek. The ground had been trampled, and in the center there were the remnants of a campfire.

Angela's heart banged in her chest, and she looked around to make sure she was alone.

Walking carefully around the outside of the clearing, she surveyed the scene and quickly realized that this was not just any camp.

Located on the edge of Denver, the Refuge had its share of squatters—homeless people who were just looking for a place to settle. The new barrier fence and stepped up patrols had put an end to it mostly, but occasionally a ranger would stumble upon a tent and some person or persons bent on living off the land.

This was not one of those cases. It was easy to see where three main poles had been set into the ground for support, and where nine more poles had been added. Someone had erected a teepee in this clearing. And, based on the look of the fire pit, it had been long ago.

It had to have been Begay and Smith, thought Angela. They must have conducted a Native American Church ceremony here, on land Begay would have deemed belong to *Tsétsêhéstâhese*, the people.

Angela pulled out her phone. The chances of someone stumbling upon the camp would've been slim. Only someone out here walking the land would ever have discovered that they were here. Sheila Henderson had been in the wrong place at the wrong time. Angela need to call Wayne, and then Tanner.

Wayne for backup and Tanner to bring the CSI.

Hitting speed dial for Wayne, Angela heard a crackling in the thicket. The phone rang on the other end, and she quickly disconnected the call and turned the volume off on her phone. Something, or someone, was pushing toward her through the thicket. Logic told her it was a deer headed for the water. Adrenalin suggested it was someone returning to the scene. There was still one person unaccounted for, someone capable of murder.

The crackling grew louder and Angela moved into the cottonwoods that bordered the creek. She unholstered her gun. Using her keypad, she texted a message to Tanner and pushed send.

The sound of a message hitting a phone sounded from the other side of the clearing. A face pushed into view. Tanner, and he was reading his message.

"Come out, come out, wherever you are."

Angela stepped out from behind the tree, as Sykes—red-faced and puffing—pushed into the open.

"What's this? A reunion?"

"*Damn*, you two scared me," Angela said, moving further into the clearing.

"Yeah? Well, I'd like to know what the hell you're doing out here." Sykes said.

"I could ask you the same thing," Angela said. Technically, she was the one who had every right to be here. They were the ones who were in a closed area of the Refuge. They should have been accompanied.

"Have you touched anything?" Sykes asked.

Angela checked her anger. Now was not the time to spar. "Of course not. I came out here on a hunch and stumbled upon the path. I was just calling for backup when I heard you."

"What kind of hunch?" Tanner asked.

"The kind she's not supposed to be following," Sykes said. "Right, Dimato?"

Her anger flared. "For what it's worth, my hunch had nothing to do with trying to connect the cases."

"Right."

"Seriously." Angela filled him in on her suspicions that Sheila had been out here scouting the homestead boundaries. "It was purely happenstance that I stumbled upon this site. But, now that we know it's here, it looks more and more like I may have been right. That the two cases are intertwined."

Sykes pulled a handkerchief out of his back pocket and mopped his brow. "I went back and talked to Begay again this morning. He tipped me off to what he and Smith were up to out here. The poor guy was spooked after you showed him the photo of that dead woman."

"Did he admit to seeing her?"

"No. And before he could elaborate, his blasted attorney showed up and told him to shut his mouth."

"Parker?" Angela looked at Tanner. "If Begay wanted to talk...."

"The attorney sicced the nurse on me. The bulldog was happy to oblige. They said the boy wasn't competent to talk because of all the pain medication, ya da, ya da. 'Boy.' Since when are you still a boy at twenty-seven?"

"How much did he tell you?"

"That they held a meeting out here on Indian land. Apparently there were a whole bunch of them here. He wouldn't name names. The rest cleared out by 6:00. He and Smith were the last to leave, around 6:45 a.m. They were ambushed a block short of Garcia's parking lot."

"Did you go with him?" Angela asked Tanner.

The deputy shook his head. "I just happened to be riding my desk when he came in needing some backup."

Angela smiled. "Low man on the totem pole?"

"Stuff it," Tanner said.

Angela turned her attention back to the clearing. "I haven't touched anything. I did take a few pictures. You can see where the poles of the teepee were jammed into the ground, and the remains of the fire."

"Let's search it by grid," Sykes said. "Agent Dimato, you take streamside, I'll walk the middle. Tanner, you take the west side."

There were lots of methods for walking a crime scene, but the grid worked best. First, they would walk parallel in one direction, an arm's length or more apart. Then, after they had marked anything of interest, they would move forty-five degrees and walk it again.

Angela studied the ground for anything that seemed out of place—a footprint, a gum wrapper, hair or fibers. They turned up nothing.

When they finished, Sykes moved to the fire pit. Bending down, he gently pushed several unburned branches to the side. That's when Ashley spotted the charred remains.

"Is that what I think it is?" Tanner asked.

Angela's stomach pitched and she fought the urge to throw up. "It's part of the eagle carcass we were looking for."

From where she stood, she could see fragments of charred bone, the breast plate with nubs of ribs attached and a partial skull. She doubted they would find any sign of the beak or talons. Angry tears stung her eyes.

"Come over here and take a picture," Tanner said, lifting the most intact portion of the carcass with a stick.

Angela forced herself to move forward and snap a few shots on her phone. Finally, she turned away and walked to the edge of the clearing. "I don't think there's any doubt now about the cases being connected."

"How do you figure?"

"It's clear that Begay and Smith killed the eagle, took the feathers, and then tried to burn the evidence."

"Or somebody else did and used the feathers to set them up," Sykes said.

"Regardless, we can agree, the feathers were taken here."

Both the deputy and the detective nodded.

"But Wayne and I found one feather across First Creek at the turn around on Chambers near the eyrie. We collected tire tracks that day."

Tanner was already on the phone. He asked to speak to someone in CSI. After a short conversation, he hung up and grinned. "They matched one of the tire casts at the turn around to Shelia Henderson's car."

"That still doesn't prove she was in possession of that feather," Sykes said. "Maybe that's where Smith and Begay killed the eagle. Maybe one of its feathers fell out."

Frustrated, Angela turned her back on the men. The detective was shooting holes in her theory faster than she could formulate it.

"Look, Dimato, it's not a bad scenario, but you have to be able to back it up," Sykes said. "Let me take another run at Begay, now that we have the bird carcass. His attorney could still argue that someone else was involved, but the circumstantial evidence of the bones in the campsite and the feathers in the car will go a long way toward making your felony case in violation of the Lacey Act. Unfortunately, you still don't have anything to go on in relation to the Henderson murder."

Angela turned around and eyed the detective. "Do you believe in coincidence, Sykes?"

The detective nodded. "You bet. I've seen way too many cases where we thought we had our man and all we had was an unfortunate twist of fate. That's why our justice system demands definitive proof before convicting a man of something as heinous as murder."

"Yeah, but how often does an innocent man get convicted?" Tanner asked.

Sykes smiled. "About as often as a guilty man goes free."

Chapter 13

After radioing CSI, Sykes had left and gone back to the station. Angela and Tanner had walked up to where her truck was parked and waited for the team.

"I don't see what he thinks he's going to find out here," Tanner said.

"The bones will give us DNA, and we can match the feathers to the carcass, including the feather we found at the turnaround. And, if we're lucky, maybe they can pull a hair or something that will help us ID some of the others who were out here that night."

Not that she harbored any real hope. The CSI solutions that you see on TV were a far cry from the truth. Most real CSI labs were outdated and backlogged. Only the fact that DOI was involved made running these tests feasible.

"What's next?" Tanner asked, putting down the tailgate on the truck and taking a seat. Angela slid up beside him and dangled her feet.

"I guess we're back to the husband." The latest stats showed that twenty-six percent of all women were killed by their husband or boyfriend. In this case there was a cheating husband, and an indication that the wife in this case knew he was cheating.

"And the girlfriend," Tanner added.

"And a missing camera." Angela remembered her conversation with Wayne from that morning. "Tanner, do you think you could get a warrant to search the Henderson house?"

Two hours later, warrant in hand, they ascended the front steps of the Henderson residence. It was late in the day. The sun dipped toward the Continental Divide, casting long shadows. The wind had picked up, but the day was still hot and dry.

Leroy Henderson opened the door. "Yeah?"

"Is your dad here?" Angela asked.

"No. He's not home yet."

"Is there anyone here beside you?" Tanner asked.

"No."

Angela turned back toward the contingent of police officers headed up the walk. "We need someone from social services before we can enter. There's only a minor child at home."

One of the officers turned back, jogged to his car and got on the radio.

"What's going on?" Leroy asked. His voice sounded small, and Angela felt badly that she was responsible for causing him stress.

"Deputy Tanner and I have a warrant to search your house, Leroy," she explained. "We're looking for a camera that your mother had with her the night before she died."

"I haven't seen it. You'll have to ask my dad."

"That's just it, we don't have to ask. You see, this piece of paper gives us the right to come inside and look around. Unfortunately, since your dad isn't here, we have to have someone come and stay with you while we search."

Tears pooled in his eyes and the look he gave her filled Angela with guilt.

"What time does your old man get home," Tanner asked.

Leroy shrugged. "It depends on how his day goes."

"Do you think you could call him?" Angela asked.

Leroy stood firm. "I'm not supposed to bother him at work."

"Even in the case of an emergency?" Angela could see the neighbors coming out on their porches. One woman held up her cell phone, likely taping the interaction. They had to play this one by the book.

"Is this an emergency?"

"You bet your—"

Angela put her hand on Tanner's sleeve. "Yes, I think he would feel this constitutes an emergency."

While Angela and Tanner stood on the front porch, Leroy called his father. She could hear Ron Henderson yelling in the background, and then Leroy shoved the phone into her hand.

"What the hell do you think you're doing?" Henderson screamed when she put the phone up to her ear. "You can't harass my son like this."

"No one has done anything to your son, Mr. Henderson. We've got social services en route. We will wait until they arrive and Leroy's out of the house before executing the warrant."

"I want to be there."

"You are welcome to come home, but we are under no obligation to wait for you to be present. Once social services is here, we are going inside."

When Angela handed the phone back to Leroy, she heard his dad berating him for opening the door and telling him to go back inside and throw the deadbolt. Stepping forward, she put her foot across the threshold.

The door swung, bouncing off the toe of her boot.

"I have to lock the door now," Leroy said.

"Don't make this harder on yourself, kid," Tanner said.

It took ten more minutes for a child advocate to arrive. By then Leroy was in tears, and he flailed around and struggled as they removed him from the house. The neighbor caught it all on tape. No doubt Henderson and his attorney would try and use it against them.

Inside, the officers fanned out. The warrant was for a search of the premises to locate a digital camera, seen in Sheila Henderson's possession on the night before she was found dead. It allowed for a search of the garage and all vehicles on the premise.

Angela was standing at the front window when Ron Henderson pulled into the driveway. Leroy was sitting at the curb with the child advocate, but Henderson ignored them and bounded up the front steps demanding to see the warrant. Angela shoved it into his hands. Two minutes later, Sam Parker arrived.

"Ron, calm down," Parker said. "Let me see the warrant." He scanned it quickly, and then looked up at Angela. "You're reaching here."

"Why do you say that, Mr. Parker? We have a camera missing that may just have the piece of incriminating evidence we need to prove your client had something to do with the murder of his wife."

Henderson blanched.

"What? I didn't kill my wife," he shouted.

"Keep your mouth shut, Ron," Parker said. "Let me do the talking."

Henderson dropped his head and nodded.

"We'll be as quick as we can," Angela said.

Parker seemed to scrutinize her, and then turned to Ron. "Do you have any cameras on the premises?"

"What?"

"Do you have any cameras, Ron? If you do, they will find them. They're going to take any camera paraphernalia and all your laptops and computers where you may have stored photos, too. You can make this easier if you just turn them over."

"It's not going to stop us from searching, Mr. Parker," Angela said.

Tanner appeared in the hallway to the kitchen, holding a camera in the air. "Found one."

The officers searched the entire house, the garage and Ron's car, and only turned up one camera. An examination showed the memory card was missing and all pictures had been erased. It was still bagged as evidence and carted away. Several items related to the camera were confiscated, as well as one desktop computer and two laptops. One appeared to be Leroy's.

"I hope you're satisfied," Parker said, once the last computer had been hauled out to one of the patrol cars.

Angela nodded. "Thank you for your cooperation."

At the front door, she passed Leroy, who dashed inside and headed for his father.

Ron cuffed him in the back of the head. "How stupid can you be, boy? Never, never open the door when you're here by yourself."

The action bordered on child abuse, and Angela considered having Henderson arrested right then and there. Instead, she cleared her throat, and gave him the evil eye.

Henderson stared for a moment, and then looked away. Patting Leroy on the shoulder, he steered him toward the kitchen. "We're almost done here, son. Go on and get yourself a snack. I'll be there in a minute."

Better.

* * *

On Monday afternoon, Tanner called.

"We came up empty," he said. "We dissected the computer and laptops. There were no photos taken at the Refuge, except for a few of the eagles in flight, nothing that contained anything incriminating. There were no photographs taken at Garcia's, either. Sorry, Dimato. Any other leads to exhaust?"

"No, not at the moment." Hanging up the phone, Angela rubbed her eyes, then propped her elbows on the desk and rested her head in her hands. Unless someone from the bar came forward to identify their mystery woman or Begay coughed up names in a plea bargain for a reduced sentence, there was nothing more to go on. They'd run down every lead and turned over every rock.

"Giving up?" Wayne said from the doorway.

Angela straightened up. "No. I'm regrouping."

"Because you looked a little despondent there."

"I feel like I'm missing something." Maybe she just wasn't ready to let Sheila Henderson's murder go unsolved, thought Angela. She had promised Leroy the morning they'd found his mother's body in that field that she would figure out what happened. She planned on keeping her promise.

Wayne nodded. "I've got one piece of good news for you. The DOI is satisfied that we're looking at nothing more than a tragic death on public lands. Unless we come up with something new for them, we're done filing reports."

"Great." *A silver lining.*

Immersing herself in work the rest of the day, Angela knocked off just after 5:00 p.m. and headed for Patty Litchfield's house. She'd been thinking about Sheila's best friend most of the day. If there was one person Sheila would have trusted it was Patty, therefore it stood to reason if she had something to hide—like a camera, or the memory card from a camera—that's who she'd go to.

Patty Litchfield opened the door on the third knock.

"Oh, it's you." She looked outside. "Do you have a warrant to search my house, too?"

"I just want to talk."

Patty looked her up and down, and then shrugged. "It's a small neighborhood. Word gets around."

"Do you mind if I come in?"

Patty shrugged again. "Why not? We can go out back."

Angela followed her through the house to the patio off the kitchen.

"You know, Leroy was pretty badly shaken up after your search and seizure yesterday. I went over there after you left. He had locked himself in his room and he refused to come out. Ron had to nearly bust the door down to get him to eat dinner."

Even though there had been little choice, Angela felt a pang of guilt. "Is he okay now?"

"I don't know. I didn't stay long. I just wanted Ron to know that I have his back, just like I had Sheila's."

"Even if Ron's the one who hurt her?" Angela asked, bracing for the reaction.

Patty reared up in her chair. "He would never do that. Even with all their problems, he cared for her. She was the mother of his kid."

"Is that why he was having an affair?"

Patty looked away. "That's just what Sheila thought. She wasn't sure."

Angela sat back in her seat. "It turns out she was right."

That got Patty's attention. She stared at Angela. "Who is it? Ellie?"

"Well, that's the thing. Ellie Parker was there, but she left early. But, we know he was there with someone." Angela told Patty how they had learned that Sheila had cased out Garcia's the night before her body was found. "That's why we searched the Henderson's house. We needed to find that camera."

"Did you?"

"No, but then I got to thinking. If I was a woman who had just snapped pictures of my husband's mistress, what would I do with them?" Angela waited to see if Patty would fill in the gap, and admit to having the memory card.

"And?" Patty asked.

"I thought she might have brought them to you, for safekeeping."

Patty looked surprised. "Why, no, she didn't bring anything

here. I went to bed early that night. The next morning, she was dead."

"Any chance she could have left it here without your knowledge? Did she have a key to your house?"

"Of course." Patty smoothed the front of her capris. "But if she'd come inside, the alarm would have chirped. I'm a very light sleeper."

"What about someone else? A minister, or another friend."

Patty made a face, and tipped her head to the side like she was thinking, then shook her head. "I can't think of anyone. She wasn't religious and I don't know who else she would trust. I was the only one she'd told about her suspicions." Patty took a deep breath, and then suddenly stood. "All of this is just so upsetting. I could use a drink. Do you want one?"

"No, thanks, I shouldn't," Angela said. Technically she was off-duty, but she was still driving the USFW truck.

"Oh come on," Patty said through the screen door to the kitchen. "One drink won't hurt you."

"Maybe some lemonade or iced tea."

"Lemonade. You got it. Ice?"

"Sure."

It only took Patty a few minutes to come back outside with two drinks in hand. She handed Angela a tall glass filled with ice and lemonade, and then took a long sip out of her glass. "Oh, that tastes good. There's nothing quite like gin and coke."

Chapter 14

Angela set her glass down on the patio table, harder than she had intended. Patty jumped.

"It's you," Angela said. How had she missed it?

"What are you talking about?" Patty said, setting down her own glass and blotting the front of her blouse with a napkin. "Look what you made me do."

"You are the one having an affair with Sheila's husband."

Patty's face drained of color. "That's ludicrous. She was my best friend."

"The bartender at Garcia's couldn't remember your face, but he never forgets a drink. Nobody drinks gin and coke without ice. Except you."

Patty dropped her napkin and her face crumpled. "You have to believe me, I didn't mean for it to happen."

That's what they all say. "It had to start somewhere."

"You have to understand, Sheila wasn't easy to live with. Ron needed someone to talk to. He would come by here sometimes, and ask me what I thought about the things she would do. One day he just leaned over and kissed me."

"What happened that night at Garcia's?"

"Ron and I had never gone out before, and Garcia's is sort of a dive bar. No one we know goes there. Sometimes he goes there with the guys after work, but just because it's close." Patty picked up the napkin and started pulling at it with her fingers. "No matter what you might think, Ron and I were in love. We wanted to be together. We just didn't know how we were going to tell Sheila and Leroy. We were trying to figure it out."

"I take it he called you from the bar," Angela said.

"After everyone left. Sheila was supposed to be home with

Leroy. All I wanted was just to go out and have some fun for a change. Have people see how happy we were together, instead of sneaking around all the time, you know?"

"Keep going."

"We were having a great time, then Ron when out front for a cigarette. When he came back, he was all upset. He said Sheila was outside in front, and that she had a camera. He told me to go out the back, while he went out to confront her."

So far her story matched the bartender's. "What happened next?"

Patty reached over, picked up her glass and took a huge swallow of gin and coke. "Sheila was waiting for me in the alley."

Angela waited for her to continue, but Patty just stared into her glass. "And?"

Patty glanced up. "She looked so hurt. I told her how sorry I was, that it didn't change the fact I loved her. She and I were best friends since grade school. I told her that sometimes friends just fell in love with the same man. That she'd had her time with Ron, and that now it was my time."

Angela couldn't help but laugh. "I bet that went over well."

"She told me she never wanted to talk to me again."

Angela leaned toward Patty. "Did she say she was going to confront Ron?"

"No. She just walked away. That was the last time I saw her." Patty took another slug of her drink. "The worst part is that, now, Ron says we shouldn't be together. He's worried about what people will say if they find out. He says he feels too guilty. Well, he wasn't worried when he was sneaking in my backdoor."

"What did you do after Sheila left," Angela asked.

"I came home and waited for Ron to call. He never did."

"Do you know if Sheila went home and confronted him?" If

so, there might have been a confrontation, thought Angela. He was a man prone to violence. She'd seen him whack his son in the back of the head.

"I don't know," Patty said. "But if Ron said she was home in the morning, she was home."

Angela admired the loyalty, but unlike eagles that mate for life, humans were a fickle lot. "You're better off without him."

* * *

The minute Angela hit the truck she called Tanner and told him about her conversation with Patty Litchfield.

"Do you think she helped him kill her?" the deputy asked.

"No." Angela didn't get the feeling that Patty was of much danger to anyone but herself. The problem was that she wasn't sure if Ron had killed Sheila either. He was like most bullies. Easy to back down, if you were brave enough to stand up to them.

"What are you thinking?" Tanner asked.

"I say let's bring him in for questioning," Angela said. "And hope we get to him before Patty lets him know we're on to them."

* * *

Henderson walked into the Sheriff's office at 10 a.m. the next morning with his attorney Sam Parker leading the way. Angela watched in dismay as they were shown into the conference room.

"I hoped to do this in interrogation," she said to Tanner as they walked down the hall.

"Parker talked to the D.A."

The two men were seated at a large table drinking coffee.

Parker stood when Angela entered the room.

"Agent Dimato. Deputy."

"Sit," she said. "Mr. Henderson, we have a few questions for you."

"Let's get to it," Parker said.

"We asked you before who you were with at Garcia's the night before your wife was discovered dead. I'm going to ask you again."

Henderson remained stone-faced, while Parker leaned in. "I don't see the relevance. That was hours before my client's wife died."

"Ever hear of 'talk and die' syndrome?" Tanner asked.

Both men turned to Tanner.

"It's when someone is struck in the head and suffers a brain bleed. Sometimes a victim can go hours before showing any symptoms."

"Mr. Henderson," Angela said, recapturing his attention. "We know that your wife had a confrontation with your mistress in the alley behind Garcia's the night before her body was discovered."

"Are you suggesting my client's mistress murdered his wife?"

"No, we're suggesting that Sheila went home that night and confronted your client, who then struck her, just like he struck his son last Friday, causing the fatal injury." Angela watched to see the effect her words were having on Henderson. At the mention of him striking his son, his face turned red and he moved to the edge of his seat.

"I didn't kill my wife," he yelled.

"Let me do the talking, Ron," Parker said.

"No, because I have nothing to hide. I didn't do anything wrong."

"You lied to us," Tanner said.

"I didn't want to drag Patty's name into this."

"Patty Litchfield," Angela said, just to get confirmation from him.

"You figured it out. I'm not proud of myself."

"What did you hit her with, Henderson?" Tanner asked.

"I didn't—"

"Be quiet, Ron." Parker interjected. "They're fishing." The attorney repositioned himself in his chair, gathering up the papers in front of him. "Do you have a murder weapon?"

Tanner looked at Angela.

"I would like Mr. Henderson to tell me what happened that night."

"And he's told you," Parker said. "He didn't talk to her."

"Mr. Parker, your client has been lying to us all along," Angela said. "First he's not having an affair, but later, when confronted with eyewitness accounts, he admits he was in the bar with someone. He won't say who, but then he admits to banging his wife's best friend. He denies knowing about a camera that's clearly visible on the surveillance videos, and then we find what we believe is the camera, in his house, with the memory card removed."

"We're done here, Ron." Parker picked up his papers. "Unless you intend to charge my client, we're leaving."

Angela knew she couldn't stop them. The case they had compiled against Ron was circumstantial at best. There was nothing substantial to back up any of their allegations—no witnesses, no murder weapon, no proof.

"Let's go, Ron," Parker said.

"Wait a minute," Henderson said. "I want to say something."

"Ron." Parker's tone clearly held a warning.

"No, they accused me of hitting my wife, but I read the coroner's report. It said there was a distinct pattern to the bruising on her head."

"Ron!" Parker's voice commanded silence.

Ron stabbed a finger toward Angela. "You searched my house and you didn't find anything."

"We didn't have a warrant to search for a weapon, just the camera."

"But if you'd found a weapon you would have confiscated it and arrested me."

"That's enough, Ron." Parker grabbed his client by the elbow and pushed him toward the door. "Don't say another word."

"You leave me and my son alone."

Angela and Tanner stood in the hall and watched them walk away. Ron yanked his arm free of Parker's grip and stormed ahead of him out the doors.

"Another epic fail," Tanner said.

"Not necessarily," Angela said, turning toward Tanner's desk. "Where is the coroner's report?"

Tanner rifled through the papers on his desk, finally coming up with a sheaf of papers. "What are we looking for?"

Angela took the packet and flipped to the appendix with the pictures the coroner had taken of Sheila. One in particular showed her head shaved on one side. A zoomed in photograph displayed a bruise with a distinctive patterning.

"The coroner said that the bruise might have been caused by a stick. Does this look like it was caused by the random marks on a tree branch?"

"Maybe," Tanner said.

"Look closer." As he leaned closer, Angela pointed out several distinct marks that were mirrored top and bottom. "That isn't a random pattern. It's symmetrical. This pattern's been etched into something. We're barking up the wrong tree. I was right all along."

"What are you talking about?"

"These markings are carved into the wood." Angela's excitement grew as the idea formed. "Begay and Smith were conducting a peyote ceremony on the edge of First Creek."

"We're back to the Indians."

"Bear with me. Every member would have had a peyote box, and every peyote box would have had a stick and a rattle marked with unique, but similar bas-relief carvings."

"Markings that might match the bruise marks on Sheila Henderson's head," Tanner said, quick on the uptake.

Angela smiled. This time, she felt sure they were onto something. "Begay's and Smith's peyote boxes have to be in the evidence locker."

It took them under ten minutes to check. Both boxes had been logged in, and both were intact. Tanner and Angela checked the carvings on the sticks and rattles. Neither were a match to marks on Sheila's head.

After talking with Sykes and learning that Begay still refused to name the others present at the ceremony that night, Angela headed back to her office. Clicking on the radio, she tuned out the music and mulled over the turn the investigation had taken. She could try and talk to Begay, but she'd have to go through Sam Parker again. He was Begay's attorney-of-record. She could contact the Native American Church to see if it kept records on peyote ceremonies, and members in the area. But, again, she'd have to go through Parker. Talk about coincidence.

Or was it? Angela sat up straighter behind the wheel of the truck. Sam Parker claimed to be a descendant of the founding father of the Native American Church, Quanah Parker. He owned a peyote box. What if Sheila had seen him on the Refuge that morning?

If word of his involvement in the ceremony and theft of the eagle feathers leaked out, his reputation would have been ruined, and Parker banked on his reputation. *Motive and means.*

Angela needed to get another look at that box. She wondered if it was still intact. Parker was arrogant, but enough to believe he could get away with murder? If she'd been in his shoes, she would have ditched the box and its contents.

Parker also took pride in his heritage, as evidenced by the display in his living room. Angela could picture right where it sat.

There had to be a way to get a hold of the box. There was no way he would let her catalog the contents now, and he had made it abundantly clear she was to have no more contact with his wife—not without going through him.

Something Ellie had told Angela niggled in the back of her mind. Ellie had said that Parker was interested in his heritage, but that he didn't have time to invest in it.

Was it possible? Had he left the door open?

Angela parked the truck and bounded up the stairs to her office. Clicking on the databases she had for the Comanche tribe, she searched for Samuel Parker's name. Samuel Bernel Parker.

No listing.

To be on the safe side, she then telephoned both the Comanche Nation Enrollment Department and spoke to the director. The woman had put her on hold and come back insisting that no one of that name was a registered tribal member.

As far as the Comanche were concerned, Samuel Bernel Parker was not *Numinu,* one of the people.

"Wayne!" Angela sprinted down the hall to her boss's office and found him nose to screen with his computer.

"You're interrupting something," Wayne said.

"I can see this. It's important." Angela realized that Wayne might not be as enthusiastic about her plan, but she needed his help. Before she could enter the Parker residence, she would have to obtain a search and seizure warrant and issue Parker a citation for illegal possession of eagle parts. "Here's what I need."

While she explained, she watched Wayne across his large wooden desk. His face expressions shifted between horrified and mild amusement. "You're serious?"

"Dead. We have every right to confiscate the peyote box, and once it's in our possession, we can check it against the bruising. Whether or not it's a match, we have him dead to rights on illegal possession."

Wayne pinched his chin between his thumb and fingers. "What level of fine are you thinking?"

"I say let's get his attention. Let's hit him with a five thousand dollar fine and one year imprisonment."

Wayne shook his head. "That will never stick."

"No, but it's a good place to negotiate from."

"I don't know a judge who will want to issue a search and seizure warrant against Sam Parker."

"He may be a powerful man, but there's got to be somebody out there that doesn't like him."

Three hours later, Angela parked outside the Parker's residence and radioed the officers in the van behind her. "Ready?"

"On your 'go,'" said the driver.

The three of them climbed out of their vehicles. Leading the way up the steps, Angela knocked on the front door. Ellie Parker answered, wearing an apron and holding a spatula. She looked surprised to see them.

"You aren't supposed to be here," she said.

"I have a warrant to seize the peyote box, along with a citation for violation of the Bald and Golden Eagle Protection Act." Angela held out the documents. Ellie took and studied them.

"This is ridiculous. My husband is a descendant of Quanah Parker. He has a right to those artifacts."

"Not according to law," Angela said, pushing past her into the house. "In order to be legal, he must be a registered member of an Indian tribe. According to the Comanche tribal records, he isn't."

Ellie followed her into the living room, brandishing the spatula. "You have no right to enter my house."

"That paper you're holding gives me the right."

The peyote box was sitting on the floor in the same spot. While Angela opened it to make sure the contents were there, Ellie dialed her phone.

"Sam? Sam, you need to come home."

Angela closed the box and fastened the clasp.

"It looks like everything's here," she said to one of the USF&W officers. "Be careful. It's old."

Ellie moved to block them from leaving. "You can't take that."

"We can," Angela said. "Now, I need you to sign here that you were served with the citation."

"I won't."

"Mrs. Parker, you need to understand something. If you don't sign, and then get out of our way, I will have you arrested for unlawful interference in the execution of this warrant."

"The contents of the box are fragile," Ellie said. "You will be responsible if anything is damaged."

"There are already two feathers broken on the peyote rattle," Angela said, handing her a pen.

Ellie stared at Angela before taking it. Her hand shook as she initialed the papers. "Sam will be here any minute. If you just wait, he'll be able to clear this entire mess up."

"I doubt it," Angela said.

Chapter 15

Wayne was waiting for Angela when she got back to back to the Repository.

"Sam Parker called," he said.

"My guess is he wasn't happy," she said, showing the officers where to put the box.

"He's threatened a lawsuit. Claims we're harassing him because of his representation of our chief suspect."

"Did you tell him our suspect had changed?"

"Absolutely not."

After the officers left to clock out, Angela retrieved the coroner's report and opened the box for Wayne. "Here we go."

She put on a latex glove before reaching inside. She knew her prints were already on the fan, and if the peyote box had been recently used—as she suspected it had—she knew too many people would have handled the items to make prints of any value. Still, there was always a chance.

"We'll need CSI to verify any findings," Wayne said.

"I know. But we can do some preliminary findings." Angela flipped the packet open to the close up of the bruise mark on Sheila Henderson's head. Picking up the rattle, she pointed to the markings on the handle and gourd. "Buffalo tracks."

Holding the rattle near the picture, the two of them studied the markings.

"What do you think?" she asked Wayne. To her it looked like a match. The bas-relief was thin in areas, and the marks weren't totally clear, but they appeared to be the same size, the same shape as the markings in the picture. "I think we found the murder weapon."

* * *

The next day, Angela called Tanner and asked him to meet her at the CSI lab.

"Wayne insists on confirmation, but I think we got him," Angela said, after telling him about the raid on the Parkers.

The CSI didn't agree.

"I can't be sure," he said. "There are a lot of similarities, but there aren't quite enough points that match to make it definitive."

"We don't have him. We're back to nothing," Angela said as they walked back from the lab to the squad room.

"Not exactly," Tanner said. "If he's convicted, he could go to jail. He's for sure facing a hefty fine."

Angela laughed ruefully. "I doubt he'll get much more than a slap on the hand. In cases like these judges tend to be lenient with first offenders, especially ones with Sam Parker's clout and alleged pedigree."

"Begay doesn't know that," said a voice to their left in the squad room. Angela turned to find Detective Sykes partially hidden behind a computer screen. He didn't look up.

"Only we can't talk to him," she reminded him, continuing toward Tanner's desk.

"That's all changed."

Angela stopped walking. "How so?"

Sykes looked up and smiled at her over the top of his monitor. "I got notice this morning. Parker has removed himself as Begay's attorney."

"Why?" Angela asked.

"My guess? Parker doesn't want his problem becoming public knowledge. He's being charged with the same crime as his client. It wouldn't take long for some media-type to point out the conflict of interest. Of course, for now, only you and a handful of law enforcement officers know that."

"What are you saying?" Tanner said.

"He's telling us to go talk to Begay."

"I'm saying, strike while the iron's hot, before Begay lawyer's up again. And before Parker realizes he's not in as much trouble as he thinks he is. If you play your cards right, Begay just might sing like a canary." Sykes ducked his head and went back to his computer. "Me? I'm trying to find out if Parker has a 9mm registered in his name. I have the feeling I'm shit out of luck."

"He's too smart to use his own gun."

"I agree. So, in the spirit of cooperation, I checked on guns registered to his wife. Nothing. One thing of interest, though. Ron Henderson owned a 9mm. He kept it at his office. It was reported stolen on Monday morning, after the shootings occurred."

"He neglected to tell us about that," Tanner said.

"Probably didn't want to bring any more suspicion down on himself."

"Ellie Parker would have had access to the gun," Angela said. "She could have taken it and given it to her husband."

"Yes, but then there's Sheila Henderson."

Angela frowned. "Are you suggesting that Sheila took the gun and was responsible for the shootings?"

"You're sharp." Sykes's grin expanded. "Witnesses couldn't agree on the height, but they all said the person who ran that morning was slight of build."

"But that would make it premeditated. What reason would she have for killing Smith and Begay?"

"What can I say? She loved the birds."

"And Parker?"

"Instead of being the shooter, he could have fled the scene, and then figured she was going to come gunning for him. He beats her to the punch, conks her over the head, and gets rid of the gun. End of story."

Angela walked it through her mind a second time, and then made a face. "As far-fetched as it sounds, that's actually a plausible theory."

"It's a work-in-progress," Sykes said, ducking back behind the monitor. "Oh, and for the record, I never told you to go see Begay."

"He's not as dumb as he looks," Tanner said.

"I heard that, Deputy."

Tanner winked at Angela. "I say let's go talk to Begay."

Angela hesitated. She knew she should return the rattle to the evidence lockup and then call Wayne. The rattle was a museum-quality artifact, and Wayne was waiting for her back at the office to give him the word on the alleged murder weapon. Of course the minute he heard that the CSI couldn't confirm, her ability to maneuver on this case went out the door.

"Onward," Angela said. "I'll drive."

***

The guard on duty at the lockdown unit told Angela and Tanner they would have to wait. "The nurse says Prisoner Begay is in the middle of a procedure."

"What kind?" Tanner asked.

Angela figured with the new HIPA rules there would be no information forthcoming, and she was right.

"Any idea how long it will take?" she asked.

Again, the guard had no answer but the rise and fall of his shoulders. "I suggest you try back in fifteen."

"That's enough time to grab a cup of coffee from the cafeteria," Angela said. "I don't know about you, but I could use one."

After locating the cafeteria in the basement of Pavilion A and ordering, they sat—Angela sipping a Starbucks mocha and Tanner wolfing down a plate of meatballs and mash potatoes.

"I think we need a strategy," Angela said, glancing around at the modern surroundings. Denver Health had come a long way from the old Denver General. Curved display counters offered up everything from fruit cups to sushi, while cooking stations offered specialty foods to gourmet burgers.

"What, like good cop, bad cop?"

"Just some way to convince Begay that giving up the names of his fellow worshippers—specifically Samuel Parker's—is in his best interest."

"Maybe just having the douche bag bail on him will be enough."

"How about we tell him we found the murder weapon and that, because we don't have the name of the killer, we're charging him as an accessory?"

Tanner talked around a mouthful of potatoes. "That would scare me."

They continued to brainstorm, fine-tuning their approach, eating through twenty minutes of time before they arrived back at the guard station.

"Is Begay free now?" Angela asked.

"Who?" the guard said. Acting as if he didn't remember her, he checked her ID again, then picked up the phone receiver and dialed the nurses' station. "Visitor for Patrick Begay. Yes, ma'am."

Hanging up the phone, the guard shoved the sign-in clipboard toward her and signaled for Tanner.

"We're up," Angela said.

"Both of you need to sign in," said the guard. He checked Tanner's ID again, then led them over and unlocked the double doors to the unit. "And this time, stop at the nurses' station."

He did remember.

The unit was busier than the last time they were there. Every bed was filled, including the beds in the overflow rooms. Guards were posted in front of most of the rooms and there appeared to be several doctors, nurses and aides on duty. Just as they stepped up to speak to the nurse, a contingent of doctors in medical scrubs bustled through a separate set of doors, forcing them to stand and wait.

Begay's room was visible from where the stood, but today the curtain was drawn. Angela hoped whatever type of procedure he had wouldn't prevent him from talking.

"I'll be with you in a minute," the nurse said, grabbing her stethoscope off of the desk. "We're being briefed on a patient that just came back from OR. Feel free to have a seat."

"We just need to...." then Angela was talking to air.

Turning away from the desk, she found Tanner already flopped down in one of the chairs. Angela sat next to him. Begay's room was hidden from view where they were seated, but they had front row seats to the drama going on in room three. Like all humans, she had a fine-tuned sense of morbid curiosity and she paid rapt attention.

Then all hell broke loose. Bells and whistles started going off. For a minute, Angela thought the patient they had just brought in had crashed, and then a nurse raced to look at the monitors above the nurses' station desk.

"Room ten," she shouted.

That was Begay's room.

One of the doctors and two nurses raced for his room. Angela started that way, when one of the guards blocked her path.

"Sit back down."

"I'm a federal officer. He's my prisoner," she said. Not exactly the truth, but close.

"Let the docs do their job." The guard was impassive, so Angela stood to the side and tried to see what was happening.

"Code blue. Code blue."

"That's not good," Tanner said.

Someone in blue pushed out the medical personnel door, and then the nurse who had told them to wait stepped out of Begay's room and yelled, "Stop that person."

Two of the guards and Angela sprang into action.

"Stay with Begay," she yelled to Tanner as she pushed open the door. A flash of blue to right pulled her away from the other guards. "They went this way."

Racing along the corridor, she realized the guards had turned in the other direction. She was on her own. Turning the next corner, she caught sight of the person in scrubs running. Whoever it was didn't want to be recognized. They had covered their hair with a blue cap, wore a mask and medical booties.

She watched as the suspect slid around the next corner and hoped maybe the fact her own boots had traction would give her an edge. Then she turned the corner and came face-to-face with a hallway of medical personnel, all dressed in scrubs.

Her heart pounded in her chest from the exertion and she gulped air as she searched the crowd.

Her suspect was tall. That eliminated about half.

Her suspect had on a mask. That eliminated three-quarters.

Her suspect would try to move fast. *There!*

She spotted the person at the elevator, and got there just as the doors closed. The suspect had kept their face down. *Damn.*

Angela bolted for the stairs. She reached the first floor and scanned the crowd that had gotten off the elevator. The suspect wasn't there.

She followed suit for seven more floor. Exiting the stairwell on nine, her heart banged in her chest so hard she thought it might explode. Her legs wobbled as she walked toward the elevator, but she knew the suspect was trapped. The doors would open and there would be nowhere to go.

The elevator dinged and Angela braced for the suspect to charge.

Nothing.

She looked inside. The elevator was empty. The suspect had gotten away.

Angela backtracked to the first floor and located the security offices. Explaining the situation, she talked the woman in charge into pulling up recent footage on the security cam.

"There." Angela pointed. On the tape, the suspect could be seen exiting the elevator on the third floor and slipping through a doorway on the opposite side of the elevator. "Where does that door lead?"

"To the walkway to the garage," the security chief said.

"Do you have a camera there?"

"We have camera's everywhere." She pulled up the security footage and they watched it play out on camera. Keeping his face turned away from the camera, the suspect walked to the garage, climbed down two flights and exited onto the street.

"Can you track him?" Angela asked.

"On the grounds," the security chief amended. "I'm afraid we lost him."

Angela thanked the woman, and then headed back to the lockdown unit. Tanner was waiting for her by the guard station.

"Whoever it was got away," she said. "How's Begay?"

Tanner shook his head. "He's dead."

"What the hell happened?" She started for the unit doors, but Tanner grabbed her arm.

"He's dead and they've locked the unit down tight. No one but medical personnel is allowed inside. They've posted guards at every doorway. We've been asked to submit statements in writing about what we saw."

Angela slumped into a chair in the hallway. "Did they say how he died?"

"Nothing official, but they believe the suspect pushed a syringe full of air into his PICC line. It caused an air embolism, which triggered a heart attack."

"Someone didn't want him talking," Angela said.

Tanner sat down beside her and splayed out his legs. "Care to take a guess?"

"There's no way to prove it was Sam Parker," Angela said. "I looked at the security footage. We never saw the suspects face. He was tall."

"Not good enough."

"You sound like Wayne."

"Or Sykes."

Or both, Angela thought. Begay had been their last hope at pinpointing who shot him, and who killed Shelia Henderson. They were going home in defeat.

Chapter 16

After dropping Tanner back at the Adams County Sheriff's Office, Angela had tucked her tail between her legs and gone back to the National Eagle Repository. Wayne had taken the news poorly, and ordered her to get back to the work at hand and let the matter drop. She spent the rest of the afternoon catching up on documenting items that had come in the last few days and processing requests for eagle feathers from members of Indian tribes across the country. With the United Tribes International Powwow, held in Bismarck, ND, the weekend following Labor Day, and the Morongo Thunder and Lightning Pow Wow scheduled for late September, the requests were thicker than usual.

Traditionally, powwows were a celebration of Native American culture and heritage, and held in the spring. The number of requests received in early-winter paid tribute to that. In the old days, they held more religious significance—a time for naming and honoring—and signified a time to welcome the new beginnings of life. Some historians believed the word "powwow" derived from the Massachusett Indian word "*pauwau*," referring to tribal and family council gatherings. The thought was that as the eastern tribes were moved west, their customs spread.

Today's powwows were different. They served more as a social gathering and carried a festive atmosphere. Indian dancers and singers, food vendors and artists traveled a "powwow circuit," most earning their livelihood during the season. The monetary payouts for coming in first in the dance and drum competitions paid in the thousands, and for most eagle feathers were part of traditional costuming. The better the costumes, the better they chance for a big payout. It was capitalism at work.

Or maybe she was just jaded.

Angela pulled the rattle out of the evidence bag and studied the markings again. She knew in her heart this was the instrument used to kill Sheila Henderson, but she couldn't tie it to the victim. Not without leaving a measure of doubt. Sam Parker was going to get away with murder.

She traced her finger lightly over the intricate raised carvings. The buffalo tracks had worn over time, but the rattle itself was a superior specimen. The beadwork at the neck near the gourd and at the end should a craftsmanship rarely equaled today. It denoted a time when it was a good day's work to toll over coiling a strand of beads onto a handle; when it was a good day's work to carve delicate bas-reliefs into wood that would span generations. Too bad two of the feathers were broken.

Angela started to place the rattle back in the peyote box, and stopped. That was it. Two of the feathers were broken.

Setting down the rattle, she dug through the stacks of paper on her desk for the coroner's report. The pathologist who had performed the autopsy had commented to her about a sticky residue on Sheila Henderson's hand that he couldn't identify.

He appeared he never had. The notation about the unidentified substance was there, but she couldn't find anywhere that it had been named.

If the rattle had belonged to Quanah Parker, it could have been used in peyote ceremonies as early as the 1880s, staining the feathers with smoke and residue from the fires burned in the teepees. And while peyote wasn't burned, history recorded that Quanah was treated with masticated peyote or peyote salve for wounds he sustained when gored by a steer—a practice he likely continued. If the CSI could match the residue on the rattle to the sticky substance on Sheila Henderson's hand, there still might be a chance of cinching a connection between Sheila and the instrument that killed her.

Angela pulled a magnifying glass out of her desk drawer, and looked at the feathers more closely. There was enough material here that they just might be able to match it.

Reaching to set down the magnifier, the glass passed over the broken ends of the feathers and caused her to freeze. These feathers were newly broken.

Excitement surged through her, causing her hands to tremble. What if Sheila had broken them off? She might have seen the blow coming, tried to deflect it and ripped the shaft. If she could match the feather tips to the feathers, the lock would be airtight.

Yeah, and then there's reality, Angela. Those feathers could be anywhere. Parker could easily have disposed of them or burned them? And even if Sheila had managed to hold onto them, the broken pieces weren't found in her car. If she'd taken them with her when she abandoned the vehicle, she likely dropped them. In which case, they were probably providing some extra insulation and cushioning for a bird's nest.

A bird's nest! The burrowing owls.

If Sheila had the feathers in her hand when she died, there was every possibility that the burrowing owls would have taken the feathers to feather their nest. The only way to find out was to pull out the nest and look. The fact it was an active nest constituted a violation of law—a law Angela was charged with enforcing.

Under the Migratory Bird Treaty Act, it was illegal to disturb the active nest of any migratory bird. To dig out the nest of a protected species drew heavy fines and possible jail time. In Colorado, where the burrowing owl was considered a threatened species, a person could also be charged under The Endangered Species Act, where fines climbed as high as $25K and six months imprisonment for intentional acts of vandalism.

But these were extenuating circumstances.

Angela glanced at the time, then picked up the rattle and put it into the peyote box. CSI would be there 24/7, but the sun would set in less than half an hour. That gave her just enough time to get out to the crime scene and check the burrow before the sun set behind the mountains. Once twilight descended on the Front Range, her chances of finding the feathers dimmed.

Angela locked up the Repository building and hurried out to her truck. Everyone else had gone home hours ago, except for a few USF&W officers. They were doing their final sweep of the park, before locking the gates at sunset.

Wayne had ordered stepped up patrols to ensure the park emptied out. Though, as evidenced by recent events, that didn't guarantee the Refuge was empty. The last thing she wanted was to get caught rifling the nest.

Sitting in the truck and listening to the radio calls of "all clear," Angela watched the sun sink closer to the purple ridge of the Continental Divide. The window of time was closing for her to work in the light.

When the call came across that the patrols were headed for the gate, she put the truck in drive. 72 was empty as she drove out to Section 5. Not wanting to leave the truck out in the open in the case a patrol wound through a final time, she pulled off on Chambers and tucked her vehicle into the turnaround near above the bridge.

Grabbing her windbreaker, a small spade and a pair of gloves from behind her back seat, Angela walked out across the field. The quiet of the evening brought a touch of coolness to the air, while the warmth of the day still radiated off the land. The light faded in increments.

The tape marking the western boundary of the crime scene flapped loose on the lathe, courtesy of the afternoon wind that had scoured the plains. Nearing the burrowing owls nest, she spotted one of the adults—most likely the male—standing vigil in front of the mound. Skinny legs supported a brown body, mottled white and topped with a round head. Its sun-faded wings were cupped to its sides like the arms of a soldier at attention. The bird turned his head as she moved closer, his bright yellow eyes over a pale horn-colored beak tracked her every movement.

The female, slightly darker in color, popped out of the mound to see what was happening, while four small heads fanned the opening of the hole.

Angela approached slowly. When she drew close, the male bobbed its head, screeched and hissed.

"I know," she said, wishing he could understand what was about to happen. "It's going to get worse."

Zipping up her windbreaker, she pulled on the gloves and wondered the best way to start. A burrow was typically six to nine feet long, descending three feet and ending in a large domed chamber. If she was lucky, she would find what she was looking for in the dung piles circling the opening.

As she moved between the male and the mound, the bird swooped past her and drove his family deeper into the hole.

Angela kneeled at the entrance. She heard the sound of a rattlesnake, and hoped it was the birds deep in the nest feigning danger. The prairie was rattlesnake country. The western diamondback rattler wasn't aggressive toward humans by nature, but it liked to hunt on summer evenings as the sun went down and it was dangerous when encountered.

The sun dipped lower, the long rays touching only the tops of the trees where the eagles nested. Angela pulled her flashlight from her belt, clicked it on, and propped it on the ground. The pale beam widened, shining into the mouth of the hole.

Gingerly, she reached inside, pulled a chunk from the dung ring at the mouth of the burrow. Gently, she crumbled the dried excrement in her glove. Each time she came upon something different, she stopped to examine the find. She didn't want to damage the feathers in the process of unearthing them.

When she didn't find them on the first pass, she reached in and removed another chunk, continuing the process handful after handful.

Nothing.

Scooting forward the reached deeper into the hole. The rattling sound grew louder.

She figured by now a rattlesnake would have struck.

"I come in peace little birds," she said. The same thing the white man had said to the Indians.

Angela didn't have to excavate long. Her next handful produced the feathers she was looking for—two white tips with broken shafts.

"We're done," she said to the owls. Not sure if they would stay in the nest now that she had disturbed it, she still repacked the dung, shaping it like a Jell-O mold at the front of the burrow. She would come out here tomorrow to check on the birds. Often the family had a satellite burrow to move to should their home become unsafe. If they never moved, it served as sort of a "man-cave" for the male who spent less time at home.

Angela sat up, carefully bagged the feathers and slipped them into her jacket pocket. Climbing to her feet, she noticed she wasn't alone. Someone stood near the road, staring out into the field.

Parker?

Whoever it was, they weren't USF&W. The car they drove looked like a newer black SUV. Angela was horrible with makes and models. Tall and lean, the figure was dressed all in black, hair covered by a black knit cap, a shadow in the quickly darkening night.

"Is that you, Parker?" she called out, picking up her flashlight and shining it toward the dark figure. The light dissipated in the night, falling short of the roadway.

No answer. His silence made Angela edgy, but who else could it be? And now she had the evidence to charge him with Sheila's murder, and to prove him complicit in the attacks on Smith and Begay, and the bald eagle.

Then Parker leaned into the backseat and came up with a rifle.

Angela's breath caught in her throat. Fear stabbed her chest and burst of adrenalin pumped through her veins.

Instinctively she reached for her weapon, and then realized how ludicrous that was. At this distance, her 9mm Sig was no match for a rifle.

Parker leveled the gun. He stood approximately five-hundred feet away, about one and a half football fields, well in range with most hunting rifles and this one looked like a high-powered model.

Run. The internal command rose from deep in her psyche and she bolted toward the trees. It's where her truck was, and both her phone and radio. She'd left them sitting on the console.

A shot rang out.

The bullet chipped the ground at Angela's feet and she zagged right. Parker's second shot tore up the ground where Angela would have been standing without making adjustment. By shot number three, she was out of range.

She kept running, unable to see the ground for the dark. Her foot caught the edge of a prairie dog hole and her ankle twisted. She felt the ligaments stretch and twist, the pain sharp. She hit the ground hard, and her flashlight bounced away.

On the road, a car door slammed. The engine of the SUV roared to life.

Climbing to her feet, Angela heard a door slam and an engine rev. Scrambling to her feet she bolted for the tree line. The pain of each step brought tears to her eyes, but she knew she couldn't stop.

At the tree line, she turned to look. The SUV raced across the field toward her, bouncing and weaving through the prairie dog mounds. Within seconds the car would be upon her.

Angela pushed deeper into the trees. The trees grew too close here to allow the shooter to follow on wheels. He would have to abandon the SUV and take after her on foot. By then, she would be at the truck and driving away.

She pushed through the grass and bushes crowding the trees. A branch swept her face, scratching her skin. Her ankle caused her to run and hop.

A shot ricocheted off a nearby tree.

The USF&W truck came into view and Angela ran for the vehicle. Rounding the bed of the truck, she noticed the back tires were flat. At the driver's side door, she spotted her phone and radio on the ground. Both had been smashed and broken.

He had figured out that she knew and what she was up to. His plan must have been to leave her in the field where Sheila Henderson died.

With no transportation and no way to call for help, she didn't have many options. Parker had her pinned down in a copse of trees that stretched a half a mile and at most five-hundred feet wide on the north side of 72nd.

Another shot drove her to move. She raced for the roost area. To cross Chambers, she would be out in the open for about twenty-five feet, but there was no other choice.

Racing for the roost area with her ankle swelling inside her boot, she barely noticed the pain. As she bolted across the road, a bullet tore through her jacket and creased her upper arm. The burn sparked a fire of anger deep in her gut. She was not going to die out here.

If he was tracking her movement through the trees and brush, the best place to stay invisible was to stick to the small trickle of water that constituted First Creek.

The water soaked into her shoes, making them heavy, but cooling the heat of her sprained ankle. The boot acted like a splint. Her arm burned. Her right arm, her shooting arm, but she could still use it. The bullet must have only grazed her.

Passing the spot where the teepee had stood, Angela moved into the thick stand of cottonwoods, willows and hackberry bushes that bordered the north-side of the clearing. She pushed deep into the trees, searching for place to hide. With any luck, the shots had been heard by the officers locking the gate. In which case, a rescue would ensue. Or, more likely, the shots hadn't registered and she was on her own.

A few feet farther, she stumbled upon a spot where a tree branch had fallen and created a natural blind. As quietly as she could, she moved into position. A large cottonwood rose on her right, the fallen branch creating a bridge and giving her a place to prop her gun hand. The willows and hackberry had grown up around, providing natural camouflage. Forcing herself to breathe shallowly, she kept still and quiet.

She could hear Parker moving toward her through the woods. Angela knew she would have only one shot. Last time she was field tested with her weapon, she'd been accurate at fifty yards. If she could hold her shot until Parker got within twenty-five or even closer, she wouldn't miss.

The crackling in the bushes ricocheted, making it hard to know where he was in the trees. Angela had a fairly good two hundred twenty-five degree view, but she couldn't see behind her. If Parker went past and doubled back, Angela was dead.

To her advantage, Parker couldn't see any better than she could. Not unless he night vision goggles.

A crack, thirty feet to the left signaled he was closing in. She held her breath and waited. Another crack. Then a dark shadow filled a gap in the trees where earlier lights from the city twinkled through.

Angela aimed and pulled the trigger.

A groan and a crash signaled she'd hit the target. Then all hell broke loose. Bullets crashed into the tree beside her, in front of her. Angela hit the ground and crawled farther away.

From her new vantage, she could see a form propped up against a tree trunk.

Another barrage of bullets forced her back to ground. If she could somehow circle around behind him, she could put an end to this.

Cautiously she moved back the way she had come, giving a wide berth to her former hiding place. She picked her way through the vegetation, flinching each time her foot caught a branch.

Angela had no way of knowing how much time had elapsed by the time she had circled around, but the form was still there, black against the gray of the cottonwood. The gun lay on the ground, within Parker's reach, but the slump of his shoulders told her he was done.

Moving quickly, she stood and pointed her gun at the back of his head. "Flinch and I'll blow your head off."

His hand moved toward the rifle, but she stepped forward and nudged it away.

"It wasn't supposed to end this way. Why couldn't you just leave it alone?"

The voice surprised her. It was a Parker, but not Sam. It was Ellie speaking.

"You?" she said.

"Who else?" Ellie said.

Angela ran the facts through her mind. Ellie had access to the 9mm that killed Smith. Ellie had access to the peyote box.

"Why?" Angela asked. "What were you trying to protect?"

"A way of life," Ellie said, her words slurring slightly.

Angela realized she was losing blood. The woman clutched her belly and groaned.

"Do you have a phone? We need to call for help." Angela moved in closer, kicking the rifle farther away and holstering her own gun.

The phone was in Ellie's right pocket. She didn't struggle or fight when Angela took it. She didn't protest when Angela made a call to the field office and requested help.

"Stay with me, Ellie." The words sounded like they came right out of a B-movie, but the truth was, she needed to keep her talking and conscious until help arrived. "You said this was about a way of life. What did you mean?"

"He didn't care, but I did."

Angela pulled off Ellie's knit cap and handed it to her. "Press this against the wound."

"I can't," Ellie said.

"Do it!" Angela ordered, moving in closer and applying pressure to the back of Ellie's hand. She cried out in pain, and Angela asked a question to distract her from the pain. "Are you saying Sam didn't care? About what?"

"His legacy. It didn't mean anything to him."

Angela thought back to their conversation at the Parker house the first day they had met. The novels on the bookshelf, the way Ellie had romanticized being the wife of a descendant of a great Indian chief.

"Tell me what happened," Angela said.

"Sam did some pro-bono work for the Native American Church. That's the first time we were exposed to the peyote ceremony. Sam thought it was foolish, detrimental to the mind. But I understood how Quanah must have felt, being cured by the healing ceremony. I thought maybe I could be cured, too."

"Of what?" Angela asked, and then remembered the picture of the small boy. "You wanted another baby."

"The doctor's said there was no reason we could never get pregnant again. Sam tested okay. The doctors pointed fingers at me, but they could never pinpoint a reason."

"So you thought if you participated in a curing ceremony...."

"That's right. I heard about the peyote ceremony that was held out here that night from one of the wives. I asked the road man if he thought he could help."

"That's why you left Garcia's early. You didn't go home that night."

"Sam was working late. I told him I was going out with friends in Denver and planned to stay over so I could have a few drinks. Everything went smoothly, until the morning." Ellie moaned and she dropped her head toward her chest.

"Stay with me," Angela said, providing a shoulder for Ellie's head. "What happened in the morning?"

"Smith was still having visions. He had gone out to the bathroom and saw the bald eagle. He shot it out of the sky, then he and Begay plucked its feathers and threw its carcass onto the fire. I needed to be at work and told them we had to leave. That's when I spotted Sheila Henderson lurking about. She had a feather in her hand, and I knew she recognized me."

"What happened then?"

"I couldn't let her tell Ron what she had seen, so I grabbed the peyote rattle and followed her. Before she could get in her car, I swung it hard at her head. She dropped the feather, but managed to get away. She crashed her car and I was sure she was dead."

"But why shoot Smith and Begay?"

"When they found out what happened to Sheila, they said they needed to call Sam and tell him what had happened. They were convinced Sheila's accident would be tied back to them. They knew the fine for killing the eagle."

"You rode out there with them?"

"I left my car in the alley behind Garcia's. I asked them to stop at my office for a minute."

"To steal Ron's gun." It was starting to come together. "You knew you had to kill Smith and Begay in order to keep your secret." Angela felt Ellie's head move.

"I'm married to an attorney. I knew when they found Sheila someone would figure it out she'd been struck in the head. It was a way to frame Ron."

Smart, thought Angela. It kept Ellie's secret, and it made it look like Ron had killed Smith and Begay so they couldn't finger him in Sheila's death.

"I almost caught you at the hospital." Angela could hear sirens in the distance. "Did Sam know?"

Ellie emitted a sound, either a cough or a bitter laugh. "Sam submerged himself at work to bury the memories of Evan. We'd grown apart."

"Angela?" shouted a voice. *Tanner.* The USF&W officers had called in the cavalry.

"Here!" she shouted.

It had taken Tanner a few minutes to locate Angela and Ellie, then a few more for the EMTs to stabilize Ellie for transport. The wound was severe enough that they called Flight for Life to transport her to Denver Heath.

"How ironic," Angela said, as she rode in Tanner's patrol car to North Suburban Medical Center. She knew the ankle was sprained, and the spot on her arm where she'd been grazed by the bullet looked more like a rug rash than anything else.

"That she's going to end up in the lockdown unit at Denver Health?"

"That she could end up in room ten, and forced to leave her Indian chief, like Cynthia Parker." Angela went to put her hands in her pockets, and remembered the bag with the feather tips. In all the commotion, she'd forgotten to tell anyone about finding the feathers.

"What do you have there?" Tanner asked.

Angela wrestled with telling him. Now that Ellie had confessed to the crimes, there really wasn't a reason to divulge her violation of the burrowing owls' nest. But it was also the final piece of the puzzle, the nail in the coffin, and the reason she was out there tonight in the first place.

"The feathers." She told Tanner how she had figured it out. "And if CSI can match the residue from Sheila's hand to the feathers, the case is ironclad."

"How did Ellie know you had figured it out?" Tanner wondered.

Angela thought back. "I think she knew the day we confiscated the peyote box. She tried to threaten me, saying she'd sue us if there was any damage to the contents. I mentioned the broken feathers."

"She almost got away with it." Tanner pulled into the emergency entrance of the hospital. "What happens now?"

"That's up to the D.A. By and large, our job is done."

Chapter 17

Angela did have one thing left to do.

Putting the truck into park, she climbed out and retrieved a pair of crutches from the passenger's side. The doctor had told her to stay off her foot, but he hadn't told her not to drive—a technicality, but one that had worked in her favor. Her armpits were already sore and she chafed at having to use the crutches, but the pain in her ankle kept her honest.

It took her a few minutes to climb the steps to the front door of the Henderson's house. Before she could ring the doorbell, the door swung open. Leroy Henderson stood in the doorway.

"Hey," she said. "Are you here alone?"

Leroy scowled. "My dad's on his way home. I called and told him you were here."

"I just want to talk."

"I'm not supposed to talk to you anymore."

Angela pointed to the swing on the porch. "Mind if I sit?"

"Suit yourself," he said.

She hobbled over to the swing, sat and put her crutches on the deck. "Remember how I promised you we would find the person who killed your mom?"

"Yeah." Leroy inched forward, leaving the door ajar. Not unlike the burrowing owl. Curious about what was going on around him, but careful to keep open the option of diving into his burrow for safety.

"We got her."

"Her?"

Angela told him the story, skimming over a few of the details. "Your mom was smart. She kept the evidence that will ultimately send her killer to jail."

"That lady almost framed my dad."

"You're right. And she would have gotten away with murder, if it hadn't been for your mom and a parliament of owls."

Burrowing Owls

Athene cunicularia
Family : Strigidae

APPEARANCE: A small ground-dwelling bird with very long legs and a small brown body with speckles of white. It has a round head without ear tufts, lemon yellow irises, bold white eyebrows and a prominent white chin strap. Its wings are rounded and its tale is short.

The male is slightly larger than the female. Still, the easiest way to tell the sexes apart is by feather color. The male spends most of his time outside of the burrow and therefore has sun-bleached plumage, compared with the darker plumage of the female, who spends most of her time inside the burrow. The owl has a life span of 6 to 8 years.

RANGE: There are two races of burrowing owls in North America—the Florida Burrowing Owl (floridana) and the Western Burrowing Owl (hypugaea). The Florida Burrowing Owl is restricted to Florida, the Bahamas and marginally southern Georgia; the Western Burrowing Owl ranges from east Texas, north to southern Manitoba, west across southern Canada and all across the western U.S. Common names for the burrowing owl include: Billy Owl, Prairie Dog Owl, Prairie Owl, Ground Owl and Howdy Owl.

HABITAT: The burrowing owls home is a hole in the ground. They especially like holes created and then abandoned by squirrels, prairie dogs or other rodents, and even turtles. The owls are usually found in dry, level and open terrain with low vegetation and available perches. The owls like to sit on fences, utility poles, posts or even raised rodent mounds. The abundance of mounds seems to be favored.

VOICE: Its voice is a soft hollow coo-hooooo, or it can make a squeaky chuckling chatter.

BEHAVIORS: The burrowing owl catches food with its feet and hunts by walking, hopping or running along the ground or from a perch close to its burrow. It eats primarily insects, scorpions, small mammals, birds and reptiles. The burrowing owl likes to line its nest with horse, bison or cow manure—probably to attract dung beetles, which it then captures and eats. When it feels threatened, the burrowing owl can make a sound that imitates a rattlesnake in order to scare predators away.

CONSERVATION: The populations of burrowing owls are decreasing and it appears on the endangered or threatened lists in many states. The primary source of mortality is collision with cars, with human activity increasing on the species range due to land development and oil and gas development.

Author's Notes

In A Parliament of Owls, Book #6, I brought back Angela Dimato, the US Fish & Wildlife Special Agent from Death Takes a Gander. Angela has been reassigned to the National Eagle and Wildlife Property Repositories based on the Rocky Mountain Arsenal Refuge in Commerce City, Colorado.

The burrowing owls love the Rocky Mountain Arsenal Refuge and it offered an interesting site for various others reasons. Originally inhabited by bands of Native Americans that roamed the land following the herds of bison, homesteaders had put down roots in the 1860s. Then, in 1942, the Army expropriated the property to build a munitions plant in the heart of the country. The Arsenal later became a Super Fund site before being designated a Wildlife Refuge in 1992—primarily due to a pair of nesting bald eagles.

Located just northeast of Denver, Colorado, is the 15,000 acre Rocky Mountain Arsenal National Wildlife Refuge. Its prairie, wetland and woodland habitat is home to over 330 species of mammals, birds, reptiles, amphibians and fish. In the spring, you can see Bullock's orioles, warblers, finches and other migrating songbirds. The prairie dog pups and bison calves are plentiful. In the summer the prairie blooms with flowers, the burrowing owls come in to raise their young and it's a great time to fish. In the fall, the coyotes are well-camouflaged, the mule and white-tailed deer bucks show off their antlers and the Refuge lakes provide a haven for migrating water fowl. And, in the winter, numerous bald eagles come in to roost, along with ferruginous hawks and other raptors looking to pick off an easy meal against the blanket of snow that covers the grass.

But, along with its idyllic setting and aggressive conservation efforts, there are other important things at play on the Refuge. It is illegal for any individual to possess a bald or golden eagle or its parts, but the National Eagle Repository, located on the Refuge, provides a central location for the receipt and storage of bald and golden eagles found dead and the distribution of their parts to Native Americans and Alaskan Natives enrolled in federally recognized tribes for use in religious ceremonies. The Refuge also hosts the National Wildlife Property Repository, which receives, inventories, stores and disposes of confiscated wildlife items that include things such as: ivory, alligator crafts, etc.

In this sixth book in the Birdwatcher's Mystery series, Angela Dimato finds herself face to face with death with only A Parliament of Owls as witnesses.

ACKNOWLEDGMENTS

Several people helped me by providing technical information for this story. My deepest thanks to: David Lucas, Project Leader of the Rocky Mountain Arsenal National Wildlife Refuge Complex. He is the head of law enforcement on the refuge, and any resemblance to any of my law enforcement characters is purely coincidental. David helped me understand the complex relationship between the various entities that might be involved in solving a crime on the Refuge. If I got it wrong, it's on me.

I would also like to give a shout out to the staff of the Visitors Center. They spent lots of time walking me around the exhibits and answering my myriad of questions.

Additional thanks to my fellow writers and friends. To my RMFW and RMMWA buddies, you know who you are; to the members of my critique group: Marlene Henderson, Laurie Walcott, Chris Jorgensen, Suzanne Proulx, Bruce Most, Tom Farrell, Mike McClanahan, Piers Peterson and Jedeane Macdonald; and to Robert Astle, who wanted me to write about owls.

Finally, thanks to Peter Rubie, who has been a huge support this year; and my family for their unconditional love.